FIONA SIMPSON

OH LORDY !

Contents

Dedication   i

Introduction   iv

I   Part One

Not My Fault   3

What a Screw-Up   9

Growing Up   15

Flying High   21

The Devil Drink   30

Kayak Kapers and Fishing Fiascos   37

The Joys of Camping   50

Murder on Their Mind   55

Beachcombing   60

Jack of all Trades, Master of None   74

Home Surgery   82

The Dutch Fetish   87

Johnty Prayers   93

II   Part Two

Acknowledgements   101

Dedication

This book is dedicated to a very dear friend of mine, Victoria Rolling. I met Torie on Facebook some six years ago. We immediately clicked, as we shared the same naughty and sometimes inappropriate humour. How we laughed. We spoke every day of those six years, sharing highs and lows, but mainly laughing. I was also lucky enough to meet her in real life. Torie has been taken from us, way too soon and has left a huge hole in many people's hearts. I have been meaning to write this book for such a long time and her passing has given me the push I needed. Life can sometimes be cruelly short.

My book is a series of true anecdotes and I tell them as if I am recounting them to Torie, on FB, as we did.

My first memory of seeing her was that she looked like the television personality, Jill Dando. Of course, because of that, I assumed she would have the accent to match, a hot potato in her mouth, all posh and well bred. It was years before I actually heard her voice on a video and was APPALLED to hear that it was NOT POSH AT ALL!!!!! Torie had a MIDLANDS accent!!!! I immediately got on to her, explaining my horror.

'NO', I told her....'Just NO. You don't talk like that! It is wrong....an aberration. I have imagined you posh, so you simply MUST be. It's like you are an IMPOSTER. So stop it, stop it now.'

Torie, true to form, quipped back, 'that's me off for ellycy-ooooshun lessons then!'

Torie was simply lovely. Kind and funny, she will be sorely missed.

Now to explain how the book got its name. Some of you, who are also friends, will already know Torie didn't talk in the first person. Well, not on FB.... I assume she did in real life, otherwise, she was even madder than I realised. She talked as Johnty, her cheeky Border terrier. Johnty was the narrator of her tales of village life and silly things that 'Mammy' had done. His daily account would always begin with....

'Well....' and ended with 'OH LORDY'. As my book is mainly about my embarrassment, sheer stupidity, humiliation and near death experiences, what better title to choose? It would also lend itself nicely to 'fifteen shades of filth', 'not my fault' or 'it was like that when I got here'.

I feel the need to issue a warning, however. This book is not for everyone. If you don't have a strong constitution, I recommend you put it down now. Read no further. You will thank me for it, I promise. If like me, you love a bit of filth, this will be right up your street.

Torie, me and my unruly 'puppies'

Introduction

People who know me well will understand that 'accident prone' would be a fair description. Fair, yet a considerable understatement. I make Frank Spencer look competent, the Keystone Cops look like the FBI. I somehow seem to court disaster, none of it my fault. I am that person (there is always one), who all the weird stuff happens to. You probably have such a person in your group of friends and acquaintances. Don't get me wrong, I am not saying it's a gift and that I am better than you. It is not some kind of delusion of grandeur. On the contrary, I believe it to be a possible genetic mutation. Something lurking deep inside me. Something out of my control. I am the one who will innocently use a cotton bud to clean my ears and end up nearly bleeding out in the emergency room. Hanging up the washing I run a high risk of garrotting myself. I break things and set them on fire. Not deliberately. Obviously. I WOULD be that person who got something, ahem 'stuck' in the most embarrassing of places and had to get it surgically removed IF I was that way inclined. Which I am not. OBVIOUSLY. The list is endless, I won't bore you further...

For some unknown reason, things are at their worst when I am travelling. Everywhere I go, alarms start sounding, automatic doors grind to a halt, buses break down. Hell, I have even been evacuated from an airport! Twice! Once because of a fire alarm, the other time a bomb scare. Neither of which were my fault.

Obviously. Yet, I kept expecting to be grabbed by my collar and blamed. You get the idea.......

'Normal' people, on any long journey, will have SOMETHING go wrong... a lost boarding pass, a wayward suitcase, a failed landing or some such thing. Perfectly ok, nothing out of the ordinary, nothing to write home about. But I get them all and more on every journey, every time. I am the Jonah of travel, friends refuse to accompany me, fear for their very lives. On the plane, despite having asked for a window seat, I will end up sitting between 'Halitosis Henry' and 'Mahoosive Mary', who will actually be spilling into my seat. Oh, and she will be crunching peanuts, rustling the bag frantically, masticating like a mad cow with four stomachs, three of which are on MY lap... Making me want to punch her in the face. Or smash it down on her meal tray. Again and again. One end of my seatbelt is A.W.O.L, no doubt lost in one of her Michelinesque folds. I am too embarrassed to ask or rummage. I mean, who knows who or what else may be lurking in there.... Her television remote? Her next door neighbours lost kitten? Red bleedin Rum?

The plane will be late, making me miss my connection. I won't be able to find my insurance papers so will have to fork out for a hotel. There will be pubes in the bed, a cockroach infestation, the toilet won't flush or worse. And it doesn't stop there, of course, it doesn't. It's not only the 'THINGS' that go wrong, it's how I manage to compromise myself performing the simplest of tasks or interacting with fellow travelers. I get into the tightest of squeezes, the most embarrassing situations. So I try my best to keep myself to myself. It's for the best. Believe me.

The latest example, was when flying from Edinburgh back to Norway. I treated myself to a nice tube of face cream in the duty-free in Edinburgh, planning to put it into my suitcase in

Oslo, where you have to collect your cases for customs clearance before re-checking in for the inland flight. In Oslo, I waited at the luggage carousel, in vain, because my case didn't turn up. Of course, it didn't. So after filling in the missing case forms, I proceeded just with my hand baggage to go through security for my next flight. My tube of face cream would get taken from me as it was too big to be allowed through. Being Scottish, I didn't want to just throw it away, so I decided to perform an act of charity. I would give my lovely cream to somebody with a case to check in. YES! I would make their day. I scoured the departure hall for someone with a suitcase to bestow my gift upon. I had this lovely warm, generous almost smug feeling. I was on a crusade! To rid my chosen one of dry skin. To make her moist again. After careful searching and selection, I found her. The one. I tapped her on the shoulder, holding out the large tube, smiling and explaining, waiting for her to thank me gratefully, maybe even give me a hug? My new found friend backed away from me with a look of horror on her face. At that moment, the penny dropped and I could actually SEE and understand what she was thinking.... that I was a BAD PERSON..... that I was handing her a tube of semtex or bleedin dynamite that would blow her plane to Kingdom come! What in dog's name is wrong with me? Why hadn't I thought of that? I shoved the offending article back into my pocket and ran away before she could call security.

I have no idea why I am like this. I just am. I always have been and probably always will be, which is why I figured it must be the mutation thing. If it only happened when travelling, I could just assume that I had done something to piss off St. Christopher and he was raining down Karma on me. But it isn't. It may have something to do with my resistance to follow rules and instructions. I simply detest them. My brain seizes up if I am expected to read an instruction manual or the like. I just can't. If, for example, I see a sign somewhere warning ' DANGER!!! STICK TO THE PATH!!!!', or some such thing, I see it as a challenge, both intellectual and physical. My mind starts to conjure up all sorts of reasons for such a warning.' Wild animals? ' I wonder. 'Erm, you're in a city', the sensible part of my brain replies. Realizing that probably also rules out avalanches, sudden cliffs and Bermuda triangles, I then step off said path to go and look for exactly what the sign is warning me of.

Trouble Brewing

I

Part One

1

Not My Fault

Before we start, I need to explain one thing. None of the following incidents, accidents, faux pas or near death experiences were my fault. I am the victim in all this. A victim of circumstance, my family, my roots. Faulty genes if you like. Plausible deniability. Everything in this book is true, with only a smidgen of poetic license here and there. Except for the illegal stuff. THAT is made up, totally fabricated. Obviously.

My parents, both at the Bridge now, were eccentric at best, mad as a box of frogs a more accurate description. I will tell you a wee story just to prove my point and so you don't think I am just trying to shift the blame for my behaviour.

My dad, Bobby, was an intelligent man. He was the first in his working-class Irish family to go on to University. He went on to work all his life as a secondary school history teacher. Intellectually, he was as smart as they come. Practically? A total disaster area. When cordless phones first came out, he bought one for the house and when taking or making a call, would remain rooted to the spot beside the console, as if still attached by a cord. When I explained that wasn't necessary, he went to the other extreme, taking it away in the car with him!

3

Complaining when he came back that 'the bloody thing' was broken.....Erm....

I used to cruelly tease him about his naivety in some areas. When the internet took hold, despite his old-fashioned ways, he decided to join the digital revolution and buy a laptop. I showed him how to surf the Net, asking him what he would like to look at and showing him how to do it. He had broad interests and together we looked at second world war history, Irish landscape photography, Rabbie Burns poetry etc. etc..

Suddenly he piped up.. 'Would they have Kylie Minogue on there?' I considered calling the taste police, but instead replied..

'of course Dad, they have everything'. I brought up Kylie's fan page and my dad clicked on to various photos, articles and songs.

'Amazing, this internet thing, that you can find absolutely anything!', he beamed.

'Isn't it just ', I agreed, as alter ego Evil Fiona took me over and chipped in,

'You just have to be careful dad. All computers are monitored by the police. If they see you have been looking at young girls' photos, like Kylie here, you could get put on the paedophile register. The cops would come knocking on your door. Could you imagine the SHAME? '

My poor dad turned white, as I coolly walked away. Later in the day, I found him digging in the garden. He was looking a bit shifty.

'I thought you would be surfing the Net, Dad ' I said innocently.
'

'Erm, no.... it's not for me that modern nonsense'. I'd rather stick to my gardening '

I didn't find out till much later that he hadn't actually been gardening that day, he'd been burying his laptop!!!! Hoping to destroy all traces of him looking at perfectly innocent photos of Kylie Minogue! The poor man was bleedin' terrified!

The funniest though is when he came down to London, 'The Big Smoke' to visit my brother Murray. Murray lived in a posh penthouse apartment, a really smart set up. The building had a caretaker, who literally took care of everything: cleaning, delivering internal mail, the building's security, even sorting out the residents' rubbish into the recycling bins. I too was over visiting from Holland, where I lived at the time and was lucky enough to witness the following...

One morning, as we were getting ready to leave the flat for the day's adventures, my brother mentioned something about the caretaker's duties, bragging about the great services the apartment had. My dad turned pale.

'What do you mean he goes through the bins? '

'Yeah, great, innit ' Murray replied. *Cue Dad scurrying off to rummage through the bin *.

Me- 'Erm, what are you doing Dad? '

Him (looking shifty) - 'nothing.... Just looking for something '

Me- 'What are you looking for? Did you throw something away by mistake? '

Him- 'Erm, no....... Yes.... No....'

Me - 'Okaaay....'

Him- 'I put something in here that I don't want the caretaker to see '

My imagination runs away with me at this point. Could my own father, who up till now has been posing as an upstanding citizen, actually be a gunrunner or a drug dealer? Surely not. I eyed him suspiciously nevertheless, as he retrieved a small knotted baggy from the waste.

Him (looking relieved)- ' Ok I'm ready to go now'

Me (haltingly)- 'are you taking that with you? What's in it?'

With much bashfulness, not looking me in the eye, he explained what he had done. And just as I do, when confessing sins, denying all culpability. As I said before, Murray's flat was a penthouse and because of the elevation didn't have the best water pressure. Dad had been to the toilet to 'ahem' give birth to a litter of chocolate Labradors' and the bleeding jobby wouldn't flush away !!!!! He tried everything....bombing it dambuster stylee with balled up toilet paper... waterboarding, it with cups of tap water.... praying to anyone who may be listening. You name it, he tried it. But to no avail. So, he saw no option other than to fish out the offending stool with his bare hands and give it a Christian burial, in the dark, damp depths of the refuse sack. Yes, HIS BARE HANDS! Why he didn't use rubber gloves I have no idea. My brother probably didn't have any. So for the sake of the story, we will assume he washed his hands afterwards. Not that it is relevant, but it would be kinda gross if he didn't... So, we left the apartment, for our day out, my dad swinging his little baggy, desperately looking for a place to get rid of it once and for all. Of course, this was at the time just after the spate of the London bombings when they removed bins from public places so explosives couldn't be dumped in them, so it took him an age to find somewhere to 'dump his dump' * laughs at own joke *

As for my mum, well she truly was nuts. The full nine yards and made my dad seem normal. I won't tell you any of her stories here, but one of her great, great, great (not sure how many greats, let's make it six) grandmother. It goes to show that yes, my parents were ''no the fu' shilling,' but my ancestors

6

were raving loonies! ' So what did 6x great granny do that was so deranged? ', you wonder. Well, I will tell you......The stupid bint only went and chose love over money!!!!!

My family on my dad's side were poor Irish peasants, but on my Mum's side 'the Fotheringhams', were people of standing. They lived in a castle-like mansion somewhere in the Scottish Borders. So, Lady Fotheringham, my great gran x 6, probably not actually titled, but seriously posh, only went and fell in love with and ran away with the commoner coachman! Because of this disgraceful and shameful behaviour, she was disinherited. So, if you think about it, just coz my nympho 6x great grandmother couldn't keep her knickers on, I am now a poor struggling artist and wannabe writer, instead of a lady of the Manor. Humph.

'Why are you telling us this?', you ask. Just so you understand, that none of the following incidents in the book were my fault. No. I am genetically challenged. Nature, nurture the whole shebang. I never really had a chance....

OH LORDY!

My dad, looking mental

2

What a Screw-Up

Let's turn the clock back a squidgen more than fifty years. Back to the day my dad got a Fiona-sized twinkle in his eye. Unfortunately, he was half a bottle of whisky the worse for wear when he and my mum performed the drunken nighty lifting that was to become me. My conception was quite the challenge, as Bobby 'junior' wasn't quite up to the job, apparently. He took much coaxing and persuading. A helping hand if you like. But to quote my Dad and his favourite mantra, that he frequently spouted (he believed that a joke or anecdote couldn't be told often enough)

'Long and thin goes too far in
And doesn't please the ladies
Short and thick, does the trick
And is good for making babies'

My own favourite sex quote is that of Shirley Valentine, who considered sex overrated.

'Sex is like supermarkets.....a lot of pushing and shoving...and you get very little for it at the end'.

Seriously though, isn't sex just the most, ridiculous thing? Is it just me, or do you too find it funny? It always reminds me of a dog humping. Let's face it, even the bleedin Kama Sutra... it's all just variations of the same thing. And how anybody can find rudey 'bits' attractive is a mystery to me. Bleedin butchers window, in my humble opinion...

Anyway, I digress. Back to my parents and the sex-fest. Despite my dad finding it hard (excuse the pun), after much puffing and panting, poking and prodding, the deed was done, the deal was sealed and foetus Fiona was conceived.

Fast forward nine months and a bit...... There I was, happy and content, all snuggled up in my cozy womb (well, not MINE, obviously). I simply didn't want to come out. I mean, why would I? I didn't know about chocolate back then or Netflix, not that they even had it in those days, so could see no reason to. And as for getting brutally thrust out of a slimy smelly vajeejay???? No thank you. Not me. No. Of course, the evil doctors and nurses were having none of it. They pinned my helpless mum down, slit her open and harvested me. Cut me out of her tummy they did and dragged me kicking, screaming and jaundiced into the cold cruel world. I was whisked away to get washed and blow dried, or whatever it is they do to newborn babies. Shortly afterwards, having revived my dad, who had passed out from all the blood and guts, they brought me to see him and my mum. He looked horrified when the nurse handed him the little bundle of joy. The nurse tried to hide her disdain and disgust that my dad did not seem to like his offspring.

'Noooo', he cried 'she's not mine!'

Suddenly the penny dropped and the nurse turned fifty shades of red, as she took a closer look at the infant. Another baby had been born at the same time, to the owners of the local Chinese restaurant. And it was 'baby Li ' my dad was holding, not 'baby

Simpson'!!! She had handed him the wrong one!

Despite not being happy about being wrenched from my lovely, snuggly womb, I wasn't a bad baby. Although, in fairness, how bad can a baby actually be? What kind of trouble can they get into with their limited capabilities short of deliberately projectile pooping on people, I can't actually think of any. But then again, I am not a mother. I haven't bred. Maybe for the best.... Babies' cuteness rules and overrides any annoyingness, apparently. Some poor mothers don't sleep for years, yet still seem to like their brats. It really is quite odd. One broken night and I would be putting mine up for adoption or selling it on eBay. Babies can do no wrong. I bet they could get away with murder and nobody would blink an eye. People would just say 'oh bless, look at those tiny wee toes', ignoring the dead body lying next to the said killer baby. So, like all other babies, I was sweet and innocent.

However, once I learned to walk and talk, it was a different story altogether. By all accounts, I was a little bitch. Hard to believe, I know. I taunted and teased my poor brother mercilessly and incessantly. I really was quite evil.

As we were only thirteen months apart, he is the oldest, my parents 'kept' us in a double pushchair. This did not work out well for my poor long-suffering brother. Not only was my victim within reach, he was strapped in! Incapacitated. Helpless. Not only was I cruel and tyrannical, I was a mini mistress of manipulation. I used to slap myself hard, on the leg, or on the face, making a visible red welt and then run to my dad crying.

'Look what Murray has done to me!' *hangs head in shame*

The poor boy would be punished and how I would gloat.

On other occasions, we would be treated to an ice cream, side by side in our pushchair. I used to scoff mine down quickly,

11

then lash out with protracted claws until he surrendered his ice cream to me. I would taunt him continuously. 'You big fat ape' being one of my favourite insults. My lovely brother was as meek and kind, as I was evil. He never retaliated from my continuous onslaughts. Until one day. Yes, one day when he was about five years old, he just snapped and who can blame him? All of a sudden, the kind, gentle boy, was transformed into a rabid, slavering psychopath!

We were camping at the time, somewhere in Germany. My dad had left a hammer lying around (probably for hitting in the tent pegs) or subconsciously to rid himself of the problem that was me, or maybe he was hoping that Murray would teach me a well-deserved lesson. I can't remember exactly what I had done that caused it, but my brother grabbed the hammer in his tiny hand and raised it high above his toddler's head. His face now purple with anger, steam coming out of his ears and nostrils. An eerie war cry emanated from the depths of his soul. A summing up of the years of torture he had been subjected to. Well, I may be exaggerating a bit. Call it poetic license or the sake of argument, but he was FUMING. All the pent-up aggression, now being released. With all his might he whacked me on the head with it. There was blood spatter everywhere. Dexter would have had a field day. I was flabbergasted and actually quite impressed. Despite it hurting like Hell, I even forgot to cry. But with Murray's bloodlust sated, he confessed to my parents and I got carted off to hospital for stitches, but now with a newfound respect for my brother.

'Did it cure me of my wicked ways, though?'... you wonder. Erm.....no.....but I chose my victims more carefully! I like to think that the blow to the head at such a tender age also caused some critical damage, which I will be able to use as a defense, if I am ever in a court of law, up-on a charge.

'Guilty or not guilty', they will ask,

'Oh, but you don't understand, m'lud, my parents were mental (I will have a copy of the book as exhibit A in evidence),

'And..... and... and, my psychopathic brother hit me on the head with a hammer. So you see, m'lud, IT'S NOT MY FAULT!'

OH LORDY!

My dysfunctional family. Not me of course....obviously

3

Growing Up

I was a solitary child, an Einzelganger. I neither had real friends nor wanted them. I was very bright and did well at school. 'Too bright for my own good', apparently. A phrase very much used about me.

At fourteen, I got a job at a local hotel as a dishwasher and chambermaid and between the ages of fourteen and seventeen, I worked thirty hours a week. I LOVED it. It was my gateway to freedom and 'adulthood' Not only was I earning my own money, I was working with people older than myself, who introduced me to the pub scene. I felt at home immediately! I quickly discovered that pints of lager, cider, or snakebite and black-currant were my best friends. Not only did I love drinking, I excelled at it! For someone so young and quite small, I could hold it well. I fell in love with its mind changing,'problem solving' charms. This was the start of a love affair that was to last twenty-five years. Needless to say, it didn't end well.

As you know, drinking takes away your inhibitions and brings the promiscuous out in you. So not only was I getting drunk, I was becoming ahem 'sociable' and getting up to high-jinks with boys. Well, men actually. I started going out with a much older guy, who worked in another hotel. I would pretend I was sleeping over at a friend's house, but stay the night with him. This went on for many months. When my parents found out they devised a brilliant and a devious plan to straighten me out, their wayward daughter. Pfffft.

It was the school summer holidays and they sent me off to a summer camp in France.

'That doesn't sound like punishment?... You think, that sounds like fun?'.

So did I, when they told me, but little did I know.... it turned out to be a fanatical religious camp for girls. In a bleedin CONVENT!!! We weren't even Catholics, for dog's sake! Knowing my folks, it was probably cheap. Well anyway, off I was packed, with my tail between my legs. It was all 'Hail Marys' for breakfast, lunch and dinner. Confession, yes, confession, like I was gonna tell anyone what I had been up to.... There was marching (oh, the joys), cross making - we had to make a mahoosive cross for some procession we were taking part in, carrying this big cross we made probably something to do with religion *nods*. What else did we do? Oh yeah, lots of praying and stuff obviously. It was all in French and all the other girls were French. They were real religious Catholics and actually wanted to be there. I am not sure what my parents were trying to achieve by sending me to a bleedin Convent, but I had my own agenda.... I spent the month trying my best to convert them, these prissy, smug, gingham-pinafored nice girls. I taught them how to play strip poker, how to swear in English and what boys looked like under their kilts or in their case probably cassocks or some other religious regalia. Oh, and how to drink, of course. I felt this my duty as the ambassador of Scotland.... I, ahem 'found' some communion wine which did the job very nicely thank you. I may not have found religion and gone on to become a good girl or a nun (obviously), but I CAN recite the Lord's prayer in French.

Notre Pere, qui es aux cieux
Que ton nom soit sanctifie
Que ton regne vienne
Que ta volonte soit faite
Sur la terre comme au ciel

Donne-nous aujourd'hui
Notre pain de ce jour
Pardonne-nous nous offence
Comme nous pardonnons aussi
A ceux qui nous ont offenses

Et ne nous soumets pas
A la tentation, mais
Delivre-nous du mal

takes bow

Anyway, I digress. After the failed Nun attempt I was shipped off to University to study French. (This too did not end well) Before leaving, however, I sat my driving test, which surprise, surprise was a farcical failure.

My dad had been teaching me how to drive. He was a patient and a good instructor, although I couldn't help but feel disheartened that he felt the need to 'hold on' when I was driving. He took me out in his car and let me drive with learner plates on. I quickly got the hang of things and confidently applied for my test. I was so sure of myself, I even bought a cheap old banger.

It was the cutest little car, a Fiat 126. Do you know them? It was canary yellow, a tiny little thing, with a small canvas flap sunroof. It was old and barely roadworthy, but I loved it and stupidly insisted on sitting my driving test in it. When the day came around and I was waiting in the test centre to be called, I got chatting with another girl who was sitting her test for the seventh time!

'You will be fine', she assured me.

'All the testers are really nice'.......

'All except one'.....

'He is a giant of a man, six foot six and built like a brick shithouse'.....

'He is a total bastard!'....

'But you probably won't get him'...

Well, that was it. My fate was sealed. Of course, I would get him. He was my destiny and sure as day, as destiny decreed, the 'Behemoth Bastard' stomped through the door and called my name. I don't know why I even bothered going through with it. I knew how it would end. However, the terrier in me was not going to give up without trying. I tried making small talk with him as we walked out to the car park, but he was having none of it. My attempts at friendly conversation were met with nothing more than an icy stare. The only words he uttered were...

'Which car is yours?'

We had almost reached it. Already his hulking form dwarfed the car into insignificance. He eclipsed the bleeding thing, making it look nothing more than a dented tin of custard. The realisation hit me. 'F*ck! Is he even gonna be able to FIT in the bleeding thing?'

I pointed out the car to him and his lip curled in disgust and disbelief. I could smell him considering whether to refuse to take

18

me in it. Muttering aggressively under his breath, he proceeded to attempt to FOLD himself into the car. Origami obviously wasn't his strong suit, so I opened the tiny canvas roof flap, so he wouldn't decapitate himself. At last, he was in. The top of his head remained OUTSIDE in the freezing cold. I prayed the test route didn't contain any low bridges, otherwise, I would have a murder charge on my hands and we were off!!!! I could hear him seething and hating. Every time I had to change gear it meant touching him inappropriately. I could only hope this would be in my favour. It wasn't. Obviously. To cut a long story short, he failed me. This time, however, I did learn my lesson and the next time I sat my test I did so in a proper car!

Having been used to working in a hotel and a real life, down to earth, working environment, I found University so immature, pretentious and annoying. This was partly due to the subject I was studying. Edinburgh is one of the best UK universities, so you get lots of upper-middle-class 'Hooray Henrys' studying languages there. I hated them. I felt like a total misfit and wanted to kill all my fellow students, which would have been inappropriate. They all had bleeding second homes, or castles in France and were stinking rich, loud and irritating. I stuck out the first year, despite my murderous thoughts, but knew it wasn't for me. I was restless and wanted ADVENTURE. This came to me halfway through my second year, in the form of a 'drop out' paratrooper (get it?) We met when I had a holiday job in a seedy campsite bar, where he also worked. I say dropout, but he was actually kicked out because of insubordination. He was all muscles, a cheeky grin and all the morals of a stray cat. He was perfect! I loved his Neanderthal way of thinking.

'It ain't a crime, unless you're caught,' being one of my favourites. Problems were solved by 'punching peoples lights out'. Such a refreshing change to all the La Dee Da student types.

So, I neglected my studies and had fun instead. After a while, fed up of having no money, I decided to throw in the towel. Instead of actually talking it through with anyone I just left a note for my director of studies. For want of a better reason, I said I was pulling out because I was PREGNANT! Thank dog it wasn't true, but it did the trick.

Why am I telling you all this anyway? Am I rambling? What is this chapter supposed to be about? I think it's about me trying to explain why I didn't become the upstanding citizen I was supposed to become. But regrets???? None at all!!! I am happy being the impulsive gypsy that I am and feel it is my true nature. Intellectually, I could easily have become an interpreter or had some other fancy pants type of job, but socially and emotionally, it sooo isn't me. I would have had to ponce about in a twin set and pearls, even wear high frickin heels. I would have had to marry a boring old accountant called Cedric (no offence to any Cedrics out there... well, unless you are boring) we would have had 2.2 children– Penelope, Octavia and Cedric junior. Cedric junior being the 0.2, a primordial dwarf, yep. Anyway, I digress (again).

The paratrooper thing didn't end well. But believe me, that was a blessing. He left me in bad debt, which was a great lesson to me. Two years of eighty-hour weeks it took me to pay it back, but I have never been in debt since. I am pleased to say though, that I have never grown out of making risky and impulsive decisions. The house where we live, for example, we bought on a whim on the internet, never having seen it or even been within five hundred miles of it!

OH LORDY!

4

Flying High

It has started early this trip... To get to the airport, it takes an hour in the car, then two hours on a bus. How hard can it be to just sit there? Just sit on the bus. I deliberately don't engage with anyone, as I have learned that this is for the best. I ALWAYS used to attract escaped psychiatric patients or other assorted weirdos on long journeys and not be able to shake them off. I used to attract them like a magnet and once there, they clung to me like a limpet to a rock. I have had to leave buses and trains before my destination on many an occasion, just to get out of their clutches. As soon as said mad person came on the scene, sometimes before even sitting down, they would be spouting their (tragic) life stories. Once, (although this time I can't really lay the blame on them) on an overnight bus journey to London, I woke up CUDDLING the poor unsuspecting STRANGER unfortunate enough to be sitting next to me. Luckily I realised before they noticed I was awake and I could perform a subtle untangling of limbs, simultaneously doing fake snoring so they would think I was still asleep. Then, after a suitable length of time I just ' woke up ' and could pretend nothing had even happened.

... Anyway, I digress. Back to the bus journey here in Norway. I was on the way to our local tiny polar circle airport, heading onward to Oslo and then to Scotland. So, I plonked myself down and got out my book to read. I love reading. Even more, I love reading and eating at the same time. Being Scottish and a tightwad, I have come prepared and have brought food with me. I refuse..and I mean REFUSE...to pay ten quid for a bleedin sandwich at the airport. Gives me palpitations just thinking about it. So, I rummage through my bag and find myself a yoghurt. I peel the lid off gently. We don't want any accidents. ...At this point, I should tell you that I am the messiest eater EVER and at home actually, wear a tea towel as a bib. But I couldn't do that on the bus. No. Wouldn't want people thinking I was 'special'. As the lid came off, the bus bounced over a bump in the road. The yoghurt lurched out of its housing straight on to the crotch area of my jeans. It would be THERE, wouldn't it...? I survey the damage, trying to scrape the worst of it off, with my spoon., but I really only make things worse, by spreading the patch. I try to assess if washing it in the bus toilet will help at all. The sink in the toilet, I mean, not the actual toilet. Obviously. At the moment it looks like *coughs*, a certain kind of ..ahem.. stain. A rudey stain. A man stain. Washing it will look like I have peed myself. What if I get stopped and frisked at security? The pat down. I mean, can you imagine? So, I opt for the original white creamy stain, possibly the lesser of two evils, hoping that as it dries up, I will be able to flake it off with my thumbnail. This operation was semi-successful and if I pulled down my fleece, it was barely noticeable, yet still suspiciously and grossly tangible. Arriving at security, I paid extra attention before going through the metal detector thing, removing coins and jewellery. I would have even been prepared to wrench out my fillings if I thought it would have helped. I would have done anything to avoid the embarrassment of discovery. Why IS it that bodily fluids are so embarrassing? I mean we ALL emanate them or expel them at some point. We would die if we didn't. Yet, there is nothing more shameful than a skid mark or *bursts into tears* something that looks like MAN JUICE on the crotch of my jeans. I couldn't believe my luck when I sailed through the scanner, without setting it off. No staring, laughing or pointing of fingers.

Fiona- 1
Humiliation -0

But this was nothing, a mere blip. Airports have always been the stage of my worst performances... my favourite place to make a bell end of myself. One of my most memorable journeys was travelling to Oregon last year to meet my friends Joan, Jan, Laurie and Vicki. Both the outward and homeward legs were mortifying, from start to finish. Oh, the shame.... I also can't quite believe that I am not writing this from a Federal prison. Thanks for that guardian angel.

Outward Bound:
Unsurprisingly, it started before even arriving at the airport. In high spirits, I got on to the airport bus with my case. Before finding a place to sit down, the bus drove off, jerking me off balance. I had the weight of the case in my hand, which caused considerable momentum and I was propelled forward, straight into an innocent old man, sitting there, minding his own business. Bad enough, yes? Even worse, was that it was my boobage that landed in the man's face. I say face.... I mean MOUTH! *hangs head in shame* The poor guy was

mortified... and possibly terrified that he may suffocate...or get lost somewhere in the vast folds of my cleavage. Fortunately for me, he was rendered speechless... literally. With difficulty, I unleeched myself and sat down with any remaining dignity I had. Arriving at the airport, in my haste to leave the bus and my victim, I tripped over my luggage strap and nearly broke my neck falling down the bus steps. Although hurt, I speedily limped off to avoid anyone trying to help me and any further embarrassment.

I decided I needed some chocolate to calm myself down and hobbled into Marks and Spencers. I absolutely love M and S food and living abroad we don't have them, so I tend to get a bit carried away when I find myself in one. I luxuriously browsed all the aisles, drooling and trying to decide what to buy, that would be allowed through security. I have had so many things taken off of me through the years, I wasn't about to let that happen again. I was having a ball. So many scrummy things to choose from. I was jolted out of my reverie by a Tannoy announcement 'would the owner of the abandoned luggage in Marks and Spencers please return to it IMMEDIATELY or the bomb squad will blast it to Kingdom Come' (or something like that) 'Bleeding idiots', I muttered, before realising I was now at the far end of the shop, fantasising and drooling over the chocolate éclairs and it was MY luggage that was abandoned at the other end of the shop! Without looking anyone in the eye, I surreptitiously sped over to the far end of the shop and grabbed my errant luggage. Scared that the security peeps would come looking for me, I sadly left my basket of goodies behind, deciding it might be smarter to check in and concentrate on getting through security without any more mishaps. For a change, I actually succeeded in not making a tit of myself either at security or during boarding. I found my seat and settled down. 'Ah, lovely!'

There is nothing like flying because it gives you a perfectly valid excuse for doing absolutely nothing productive, for hours on end. My favourite plane activities are reading, snacking and sleeping. So that is what I did. All relaxed and content, my head resting on my coat, on the meal tray thingy. I woke up as the plane started its descent. Immediately I could see something was wrong. Well, I say 'I could see', but that was the thing....I couldn't! My right eye was almost blind! Really, really fuzzy and blurred. WTF!!!! I rubbed my knuckles in my eye, hoping that there was just something in there that needed dislodging - some airborne detritus that had infiltrated me as I slumbered. But it made no difference at all. And then the fear hit me! Sudden vision disturbance??? ... I was having a bleeding stroke!!!!!! My heart skipped a beat, then started racing like a mad thing. What the actual f ***? Could it be a heart attack? Or a deep vein thingy???? My imagination ran riot. I was cruelly laughed at afterwards, by my evil 'twin' 'deep vein thrombosis 'she mocked! 'I've been on longer bus rides!!!! It's not even two hours in the plane to Iceland' (that was where the transfer was).

But of course, being British, despite actually truly thinking I was dying, I didn't want to make a scene, so I just necked a Valium and hoped for the best. I just sat there with my eyes closed, trying to bleedin Zen myself, which ain't easy when you are convinced you are pegging it. However, after what seemed like a lifetime, the plane landed and my heart slowed down a bit but was still nowhere near normal. It took about half an hour for that to happen, the same for the miracle.... 'what was the miracle ?' You ask. My eyesight returned! Yayyayayyyay! Maybe I wasn't going to peg it after all. I soon forgot all about it. I found out later that it was most probably a side effect of 'discontinuation', as a result of trying to come off my 'mad meds'. Don't worry, though, I am back on them. It's for the best. For me and the rest of the world, yep.

I slept pretty much all through the transatlantic leg of the journey, thanks to 'Auntie Valium, so nothing untoward happened. I am at my best tranquilised. But, the untoward was in the post.....The 'fated' return journey. All I can say is that I am extremely lucky I am not writing this from a Federal prison, or Guantanamo bleedin Bay.

Going Home:

I had an amazing week with my friends in Oregon (Joan, Jan, Laurie and Vicki). It was my first time Stateside and they did everything to make sure I got the full-blown experience. It was non stop fun. So it wasn't until the last day that my host's husband got round to showing me his considerable gun collection. It included an antique rifle that his Great Great Great Grandfather had owned and actually used while travelling on the Oregon Trail. One of the things I had always wanted to do was shoot at tin cans in a canyon. Heaven knows why. When I mentioned this, my host's eyes lit up. Coincidentally, they lived on the edge of a canyon. He grabbed a few of his favourite guns from his arsenal, a selection of revolvers, pistols and rifles.

'Here Y'all are', he drawled, filling my hands with the biggest bullets you have ever seen.

'Put 'em in your pants pockets, pardner. Yeeeeehaaaaaaaw'

He plopped a Stetson on me bonce and off we went down the canyon, me looking all sexy in the Stetson, my pockets bulging with ammunition. He showed me how to shoot all the different guns. I felt like a true cowboy. It was the bestest fun. Unfortunately, though, all good things come to an end and we had to head back, as my plane was leaving in just a couple of hours. Back at the house, I quickly grabbed my bags and tearfully waved goodbye. My hosts looked suspiciously relieved that my sojourn had come to an end.

At the airport, I made sure I checked my hand luggage extra thoroughly, as I knew that American airports were especially strict. There were armed security peeps everywhere, keeping an eye on things. 'Shit !!!' I had forgotten to put my toilet bag in my suitcase, which was now checked in. So I had to throw away all my toiletries and sun cream. I wasn't a happy puppy, as you know what a tightwad I am. Just as I was approaching security, I suddenly thought...

'Oooh, better check I don't have any loose change...don't want to be setting off the metal detector.' *pat pat*

'OH, MY FRICKIN DOG NOOOOOO !!!!!'

The bullets!!!! They were still there!!! In all their gunpowdery glory!!!! What on earth was I going to do????? I felt my heart pounding in my chest, the sweat breaking out all over. I backed away from the security area, trying not to draw attention to myself. I could feel the armed guards' eyes boring into me and I still had no idea what to do. All of a fluster, I returned to the bin where I had dumped my toiletries, thrust my hand into my pocket and tossed the ammunition into the bin !!! Fully expecting to be grabbed in the back of my neck, I returned to security and put my hand luggage on the belt. I put on my bestest sweet and innocent face and hoped for the best. As I went through the metal detector, the bleedin thing went off!!! I nearly died. Had I missed one of the bullets? Please no. I was taken aside and patted down. Fortunately, there was nothing to find, it must have been a random check. But my troubles weren't over yet. I was also given the test for explosives!!! With that funny, light thing!!! I was now in full paranoia mode! What if they could detect the gunshot residue, I was surely covered in? I had started praying at this point, convinced I was doomed. I couldn't believe my luck when I was cleared to go. The relief was overwhelming. I wasn't going to prison after all yayyayayyayy!!! But my relief was short-lived, as my paranoid brain conjured up two possible, equally frightening scenarios that could have devastating consequences for me...

1. When the bin with the offending bullets got emptied, the bag tossed into the incinerator, the bullets would go off and kill everybody in the room.

Consequence - Murder one... life imprisonment without parole??? Or Old bleedin Sparky ???

2. My host decides to commit a murder, with one of the guns I had used, putting me in the frame, as my bleedin fingerprints would be all over it.

Consequence - Murder one...life imprisonment without parole??? Or the death penalty

*sighs *

OH LORDY!

Airborne Missile

5

The Devil Drink

This chapter is likely to go on to become a book in its own right. There is sooooo much material on this subject, all hideously shameful and mortifying, spanning twenty-five years. *hangs head in shame* (I do that a lot) But not as much as when I used to drink, thank dog. I think quite possibly if you put together all the booze I have consumed in my lifetime in one place, it would probably cause a tsunami. I am not saying I was an alcoholic. I don't like that word. But I drank a lot and not always for the right reasons. I self-medicated. In my twenties I developed hideous lower abdomen pains, which the doctors told me I was imagining. It took me three years to get taken seriously and at last, operated on. My appendix was chronically infected and the surgeon said I had been a walking time bomb. During this time, I used alcohol as a painkiller and of course, it went on to cause problems of its own.

I have been on the wagon for nearly ten years now and don't miss it at all. Days of waking up with that sinking paranoid feeling 'What the hell did I do last night?

Drinking to excess causes blackouts. If you are lucky, you just literally black out and fall asleep. Other less fortunate times your sodden brain just carries on embarrassing you, by performing unremembered, uncensored, acts of shame and embarrassment. No inhibitions whatsoever, you say and do the stupidest things....

I tried to be good most of the time. I even developed my own chart/scale of drunkenness, vowing never to be more than a '3'. It was based on the common term for being very drunk 'paralytic' Here goes....

Stage 1 -' stubbed toe ' -just the slightest bit tipsy

Stage 2 -' broken leg -getting loud and annoying

Stage 3 -' lower lumbar paralysis'- slurring, swaying, losing inhibitions Stage 4 -' quadriplegic'- lifting strangers' kilts, promiscuity, total ridiculousness.

Stage 5 -*'locked in syndrome' -propositioning lampposts, out of control, the stuff you forget, or definitely want to forget, illegal, immoral, il-everything-stuff.

*you know that hideous thing where you can only move your eyes, yet are aware of everything.

As you know, alcohol consumption causes you to lose your inhibitions, so that's when the most embarrassing things happen. My inhibition button is faulty at the best of times, so for me, stopping drinking was the best decision of my life. I will, however, share a few toe-curling, cringy tales with you.

As bad as it was, I don't believe in having regrets. I have done a lot of stupid things in my life, but I believe they were necessary to make me the person I am today. Not that I am good at learning from my mistakes. On the contrary.

I remember one particularly good example when I was about twelve years old. I was on an 'outdoor' weekend arranged by the school. One of the activities was hill walking. The instructor explained to the class, that there were two simple, but very important rules that had to be adhered to. One was to stick to the path at all times. The second was never to RUN downhill. I saw (and still see) rules as some kind of a challenge, like being told 'game on', my competitive spirit only wanting to win. So, the first thing I did, when we reached the top of the hill, was to separate myself from the group and start running. It was the greatest feeling to start with- the rush of speed, wind in my hair, total freedom. Until, of course, momentum took over. Suddenly, my legs were moving so fast, my body couldn't keep up. I was on a collision course, now no longer able to stop. There was only one way it could end and of course, it did - me in a crumpled heap, having tripped and rolled, arse over tit, time and time again. I came to, with the instructor, standing over me shaking his head. He then went on to make an example of me. But did I learn from this? Erm...not really, no.

I have been addicted to lots of things through the years, good and bad. Sometimes several at one time. Again, obviously not my fault, I must have an addictive personality, so it's my stupid genes again. What's a girl to do? I either have been or still am addicted to booze, fags, chocolate, papier mache, crochet, exercise, abstinence, fishing, all sorts. The fact that I can be addicted to both booze and abstinence makes me wonder if I am bipolar. Not that it would be my fault. Obviously. But, anyway, I digress (again) We were talking about drinking. One of my most shameful incidents was the following...

I must have been about nineteen, or twenty. It was sometime after the running away from University thing. Quite probably after the D-head ex-paratrooper, I had been going out with left me. Not that I was bothered about THAT, believe me, it was a relief. But what DID bother me, was that he had left me in considerable debt. Muggins here had signed credit agreements because his credit rating set alarm bells off. In a way, it turned out to be a good thing because after two years of really hard work, having cleared the debts, I have never owed anything ever again.

Ok, enough of the boring stuff... Suffice to say I was looking for a job. I had done a fair bit of bar work and decided to just show up at bars and pubs I liked in Edinburgh and ask if there was any work going. This was very thirsty work as you can imagine, trailing about from pub to pub, on a hot sunny day. Who could blame me for seeking some refreshment? Each pub I went to, I was met with disappointing news. There was either no work going, or the manager wasn't there to speak to. Not only did I have a thirst to quench, but I had rejection to deal with. A swift beer after each enquiry seemed the way to go. Initially, the alcohol fuelled my enthusiasm and loosened my tongue, yet still to no avail. Maybe the pub owners had me down for a lush and wouldn't have employed me anyway, fearing for their stock. After a while, even I realised that I was no longer entirely sober, so to avoid making a complete tit of myself decided enough was enough for the day. Enough job hunting that is. Not beer. Obviously. So after my final let down of the day, I settled myself in a 'snug' with a fresh pint. A reward for all my efforts. Tomorrow was another day I would try again then.

Well....don't ask me how long I had been sitting there, or even what time it was, but I was approached by a friendly looking bloke who offered to buy me a drink. Best chat up line in the world, in my humble opinion. Who was I to say no? He returned with the drinks and a couple of packets of crisps, which earned him extra points and we got chatting.

As luck would have it, he only had a bleedin job for me!!!! He was the head chef on a container type ship that sailed back and forth between Scotland and Scandinavia. They were looking for a trainee chef to join the team! We got on like a house on fire and spent the next few hours chatting about the job and other things. Oh, and drinking.... obviously. He suggested I come down to see the boat next week, as they were to be heading off for Scandinavia in the wee small hours. But I was drunk and overexcited and slurred...

'But I wanna see it now!!! I know I am gonna lurrrrve it!!!! Pleeeeeze!!!'

'Well, if you are sure...' he replied reluctantly.

And off we went. I was staying with my parents for a short while at this time, waiting with getting my own flat once I knew where I was going to be working. My sozzled brain forgot to get me to phone them and let them know what was happening. They were expecting me back in the afternoon.

It was dark by now, so I can't really tell you what the boat was like, except that it was huge. I managed to get on board without falling off the gangplank, surprise, surprise and he took me down to the crew's quarters to meet the rest of the staff. Everybody was so friendly and welcoming. It was like one big happy family. They were sitting around a table, playing cards and invited us to join them. Dog knows how much I had to drink by this point. Suffice to say my memory is very shaky and I may be missing a few hours. Also, there may have been.. ahem... Untoward behaviour. Don't judge me now! You have been there too, haven't you? My inhibitions had gone right out the porthole, but the huge quantities of booze were also making me very sleepy. At some point, I conked out or blacked out, or whatever.

What must have been hours later, I woke with the hangover from Hell? My head was banging and clunking and throbbing.

'Wait a minute!'It wasn't just my head. It was the ship that was making a God awful commotion. The bleeding engines had started !!!! What the actual feck????? If the engines were turning, that must mean that it is SAILING!!! I jumped up quickly and desperately tried to find my shoes! I couldn't believe it. We were on our way to frickin Scandinavia and I had nothing but the clothes I was wearing, no passport, no nothing. I wasn't part of the crew. I had yet to have a proper interview and had no doubt made such a fool of myself the previous evening that I wouldn't get the job anyway. So basically, I was nothing but a stowaway! I was dizzy and disorientated but determined to get off the ship, even if it meant jumping overboard. I turned to my.. ahem ' friend' for help, but he didn't want to get into trouble, so eased his conscience by thrusting forty quid in my hand, for a taxi, as the trains would not be running at this time. You can imagine how being 'paid' made me feel! But there was no time for that now. It turned out we were in the bowels of the ship, so I swiftly ran up a series of narrow metal staircases until I found myself on the deck.

OH MY FRICKIN DOG !!!!!!!!!!!!!!

My worst fears were realised. Looking overboard, I could see that we were no longer in the relative safety of the harbour. We were actually at sea!!! The land was visible, but certainly not swimmable. What the f*ck was I going to do. I was gonna have to fess up. There was nothing else for it. I made my way to the Bridge, with my tail between my legs and was met by the Captain's icy stare.

'Who exactly are you? ' he demanded.

There was nothing for it but to tell the truth. The shameful truth. The disgust was visible all over his face. He looked at me like I was a two-bit whore, which is exactly how I felt. Once I finished my tale of woe he turned to me and said

'And what EXACTLY would you like me to do about it?'

'Take me back, please. PLEASE '

'Have you any idea how much that will cost....how this affects our arrival time?'

I could feel the tears welling up, tried desperately to contain myself. I was terrified he wouldn't comply or actually charge me for my illegal passage....or turn me over to the Police. He let me stew for a while before slowly turning the ship around. He made me stay all the way back, alone with him and his disdain on the Bridge. It seemed to take forever. I don't think I had ever felt shame that deep up until then. I would like to be able to say that I never have since then, but that would be a lie. At last, we were back and I could leave the ship and return to the safety of dry land. Eventually, I got back to my parent's house. They were understandably fuming. They had been so worried, they had even called the Police! Whoops! I vowed never to drink again..... Until the next time....

OH LORDY!

6

Kayak Kapers and Fishing Fiascos

You know how women's body shape is sometimes described as 'apple' or 'pear'? Well, since middle age got its claws into me, I felt that 'watermelon' was a closer description of my frame. There was nothing else for it, I decided to try running again. I used to be very sporty indeed, played squash or hockey every day. But as I have grown older, my fitness has declined, in direct proportion to the growth of my front bumps. What is that all about? Hormones?????? Karma for something I have forgotten I did???? I have no idea why or how this has happened, but it has. My dad, in his subtle, nuanced way, once took a look at me and exclaimed,

'That's enough to make a baby cry!'

All I know is, that it makes running a challenge. Kind of like trying to jog while holding a litter of unruly puppies. But I am a terrier by nature and refuse to let that or them get in my way. I had read somewhere that interval training was the best way to start up. I assumed that meant having a days wait between short, bouncy stomps, but that's not what it is apparently. It's running a bit, then walking, then running again. The idea is to build it up so that you are running more and walking less. I knew there would be a catch. But hey ho, if that's the way to go....Anyway, I am making considerable progress. Now, if somebody sees me, they no longer ask if I am alright, or call an ambulance. I am also down to two chins and my jowls, no longer applaud, so it must be good for something.

I have invented a few ditties to chant while running to stop me fantasizing about deep fried mars bars (hey, I'm Scottish, don't judge me) One is 'ten unruly puppies', sung to the tune of 'ten green bottles', another 'bouncing, bouncing, bouncing, keep them puppies bouncing', sung to the tune of Rawhide. A third 'wibbly, wobbly, wibbly wobbly, jelly on a plate'. Thank heavens the snow has arrived now, here in Northern Norway, so I can cease the charade without a guilty conscience. Instead, we have made a makeshift gym in the attic of the house. Far away from prying eyes, I can bounce away to my heart's content. But I may have to face the truth that my dream of running the London Marathon will never come true. However, I care not, because this summer I developed a new and wonderful addiction!

Do you develop an addiction? Or catch one? Grow one??? I don't know, but it's not important. Shall I tell you what it is? It's FISHING!!! And more specifically, kayak fishing. I absolutely love it! But it too has come with its own mishaps and disasters. Let me tell you how it all began...

Well... my 'twin' Kait bought a kayak and flaunted it in front of me on facebook. She looked like she was having the bestest fun ever and I was so jealous it HURT! I didn't have enough money to buy one at the time, so I opted for a cheap inflatable kayak. It sounded like a good idea at the time. I counted the days until it arrived and as soon as it did, I pumped it up, tucked it under my arm and rushed off to the nearest lake. I did not let the fact that it looked like a lilo (a child's toy) dampen my spirits. I had convinced myself that it would be a professional vessel, despite all evidence to the contrary. I laid it down in the shallows and made to get in. This was not as easy as it sounds. Despite being pumped up as hard as possible, it remained a bit floppy. Also, it was designed for two people to sit in, one at each end. This I had also not taken into account. I stepped into the back of the inflatable causing the front end to lift out of the water and to propel ME into it! *SPLASH*

'Ok, practice makes perfect' I muttered to myself.

I surfaced, shaking myself like a dog and gingerly tried again. This time I actually managed to plonk myself down IN the boat. Yayayyayy. However, as I tried to paddle away, nothing happened. The water was too shallow and me lardy arse was pushing the rubber down into the bottom of the lake. I must have looked like a bleedin beached whale. So, instead of paddling, I used the cheap plastic paddle to push myself off the sand and into the deeper water. Apparently, the paddle wasn't designed to be abused in this way and the frickin thing snapped in two! My language was ripe at this point, as I had to repair the stupid thing before I could set off on my maiden voyage. I fashioned a rough splint, with a stick and some duct tape and was then ready for 'take three'. This time I waded the inflatable in deeper first, before getting in, so I could use the paddle properly. And I was off! The front of the kayak was sticking out ridiculously high, but at least I was floating. Paddling, however, appeared to be a bit of a problem. Because all the weight (me) was at the back of the boat, the front was getting caught by the wind. Instead of me being able to move forward in the water, it took all my strength just to keep the bloody thing straight and not be blown around in circles like some kind of mental maelstrom! What an absolute joke! This thing wasn't a kayak, it was a toy! I soon decided to admit my mistake. Being a cheapskate again had given me my deserved Karma.

Do you believe in Karma? Unfortunately, I do. I hope I am wrong, I truly do. Guaranteed to come back and bite you in the bum, I believe Karma is out there waiting for all of us. Dog knows what it will have in store for me. I am sure my fear of flying was Karma reigned down on me for laughing at a friend who felt claustrophobic and asked her husband to open a window in a plane. When he told her plane windows don't open (you silly bitch), she had a full-blown panic attack. How I laughed and mocked. Also, considering one of my childhood 'hobbies', was making people pee themselves and cruelly taunting my brother for being 'a big fat ape', I hardly dare imagine what is waiting around the corner for me. I will no doubt become vastly incontinent and drown in my own pee. I will be six hundred kilos, confined to my reclining chair, literally stuck in it. I will have to get removed from the house by the fire brigade and buried in a quarry. This is my future. It's what I deserve. Me and my big mouth...Anyway, I digress yet again....

Despite the inflatable being pants, it had given me the taste for kayaking. There was nothing else to do, but save until I could afford a proper one and that is what I did. I managed to justify the expense by thinking 'it's just the initial layout of four hundred pounds... after that the kayaking itself costs nothing...' This couldn't have been further from the truth. Twelve months down the line, it has cost me two cameras, two phones, one fishing rod, a baseball cap, oh and nearly the kayak itself. 'How does one write off a kayak', you wonder. I would too. *rolls eyes* The only thing I haven't done yet is to capsize, but you and I know it's only a matter of time..... Instead of recounting each individual calamity, I will group them together as a kayaking clusterf*ck. Here goes...

My beautiful new kayak had arrived! It was bright yellow, like a huge plastic banana and sported a special hole to put a fishing rod in. Feeling very much like Davy Crockett, I set off. Being a real kayak, I now wouldn't be confined to lakes, I was seaworthy! ...Well, my kayak was, me not so much.

The Kayak of Kaos

The actual kayaking I was really good at! The only real incident when in full flow was when I hadn't spotted a large underwater flat rock, which I proceeded to mount. Yes, mount. I was stranded on top of it, stuck like a limpet, could neither go forward or backwards, much to the amusement of a couple walking their dog on the shore. That, by the way, is the strangest thing. We live in the middle of nowhere, far up above the polar circle. I can be out for hours and never see a soul. Yet when I do something stupid, there is ALWAYS an audience, stifling giggles, pointing and staring. What is that all about?

So it wasn't the kayaking itself that was the problem. Oh, hang on. There may have been one more incident. Yes. It was the first time I took my rod along. I had absolutely no idea what I was doing. I cast my line in and saw another kayak nearby, a man who was also fishing. I thought I would ask him for some tips. I paddled up to him, my line still in the water and struck up a conversation. I hadn't mastered the art of keeping still, however, and somehow I managed to get MY line tangled up in his. He was not impressed, so I desperately tried to untangle us. What with the boat's movement and my fecklessness, I was only making things worse. I had now somehow managed to get myself tangled up too. I was trussed up like a bleedin rolled brisket. Desperate times called for desperate measures, so I grabbed my fishing knife and cut through my line. Sometimes running away is the best option, so that's what I did, Davy Crockett stylee.

The real challenge lies in getting in and out of the bleeding thing. The water is fricking freezing, so keeping your feet dry (and the rest of you) is very important. I have lost count of the failures. I am not 25 anymore and although I am relatively nimble, my balance is pants. (I blame the 'mad meds') Even in still water, the kayak tips one way and then back again as you enter or leave. It would have been bad enough if it was only ME getting waterboarded, but no. In the course of the year two cell phones and two cameras have found their watery grave. Oh, and my fishing rod. I tried to get in the kayak at the same time a mahoooosive wave was breaking on the shore. It flipped the kayak and me right over on our heads, snapping the rod in two! There I was floundering in the crashing waves, unable to get up again, due to the incessant waves and the drag from beneath.

The beaches here are always empty. Always. But not that day, oh no... Of course, I pretended that I had MEANT it to happen and that I WANTED a pre-fishing dip. Like anyone in their right mind would voluntarily swim in these freezing arctic waters. I remember when we first moved here, I saw someone stripping off on the beach and solemnly walking out into the sea. I almost ran up to them crying.....

'Noooooo, don't do it!! You must have something to live for!!!!', thinking it was a suicide thing.

But the funniest fishing memory must be the lardy arse incident......

(At this point in time I was seriously addicted to fishing. I was completely hooked!)

laughs at own joke

The thrill of feeling your rod getting jerked down by something is like no other. You don't know what is on the other end it is incredibly exciting. I HAD to stay out until I caught something I just had to. This day I was trying out a new fjord. I plonked myself down in my kayak and paddled off to the deepest part of the fjord and cast in. Suddenly I started feeling cold and wet. I looked down and there was a layer of water in the bottom of the boat. At first, I just assumed that I had been splashing a lot, but the level continued to rise! F*ck! I must have sat my lardy arse down too hard and there was a rock or something that punctured the boat. A normal person, having discovered this would turn around and head back to shore. But not me, oh no. I had fish to catch.

The water was up to my knees by now and making me want to pee. Because of the weight, the boat was getting harder to paddle. But, I had a fish on! Yayyayayayay !!!

Ignoring my imminent death by drowning, I happily reeled

in a beautiful stripey mackerel! The water level was higher still. I was going to have to do something. I had no idea how big the hole or split was in the boat, but the water was coming in fast and furious and I didn't have anything to empty it out with. My first genius idea was to use one of my wellies. My legs, however, were so cold from the icy water that I could no longer bend my knee properly and my attempts to remove my wellie were causing the kayak to wobble dangerously. Then my second genius idea struck me! I knew what would save my life! Rescue me from my perilous situation! My yoghurt! Yes, I had a small pot of yoghurt with me. I fished it out of my drybag, which I later discovered was a lying, cheapo, piece of sh*t, coz everything inside it was soaked (I think this was the demise of camera 2... R. I. P). I proceeded to neck the contents and just before my imminent sinking, I started using my tiny receptacle to bail me out. It took forever, but it worked. I alternated paddling and scooping and slowly made my way back to the shore with my disabled craft. I could hardly get out of the bleeding thing when I got to the shore as my muscles had seized up. But the story has a happy ending, as my hero Willem, managed to fix the gash for me, in return for ministrations. Obviously. I now make sure never to forget to take a lifesaving yoghurt along with me on expeditions.

Sushi Simpson

But the absolute worst kayaking catastrophe was the ahem 'bran affair'. When I told my editor Geordie MacBagpipe I was going to include it in the book she was horrified.

'Nooooooo!!! She said, 'you can't write that! It's gross!!!!'

'But the reader's will expect nothing less' I retorted.

'But it's all about poop!' she continued

'As are most chapters ', I muttered under my breath.

She hadn't read the book at this point, so was in for a surprise.

('Geordie is a funny name for "a she" you are thinking, maybe?) Well, that's coz, it's not really her name. It's her dog's name. I call all my friend's by their dog's names. It's a great idea, you should try it. It saves a lot of brain space, coz you only need to remember one name instead of two.) Anyway, I think I may be blabbering again...

Where were we? Oh yes, the bran... OH, MY ABSOLUTE GOOD DOG! Have you tried it? Bran? Have you? Well, if you have, you will know EXACTLY what I am about to describe. If you haven't, don't. Just don't. Not unless you have a toilet fetish and don't mind spending the rest of your life on it. I swear it should come with a Public Health Warning. It somehow makes your sphincter pucker up like a cross between a botched Botox job and a baboon. Why it puckers, I have no idea. It's not as if anyone is planning on kissing it. I can only assume, it is adopting a state of readiness *nods* And once puckered, there is no stopping it. No, Siree! You literally go from being an autonomous human being, to a slave of your own bowel. It is all-encompassing and simply terrifying. I swear you can go from blobby to anorexic in one sitting.....

Hang on a minute! Can you keep a secret? I have just had the weirdest thought.... I maybe shouldn't even mention it... I mean, if it got into the wrong hand's Dog knows what could happen...It could be the end of the world as we know it! Oh, what the Hell. I have started now, so might as well tell you. Just don't go telling' anybody else ok? Up until now, its qualities have only been lauded by nutritionists.

You know the whole 'war on terror' thing? Well, what if, instead of farting about with suitcase bombs, suicide vests, Semtex, ricin and the like, what if, the bad guys stumbled on the idea of ' Bran, the husk of mass destruction'? It could disable the whole bleeding nation within hours! One minute everyone would be going about their normal, productive lives and the next they will be doubled over in agony and running for the nearest toilet, praying they will make it in time. Everything would grind to a halt because they would be terrified to leave! The stock market would crash and the nation would fall. The scariest thing is, that just anybody could walk into a supermarket and buy some! Maybe I should patent the idea and sell it to the Government so they can launch a preemptive strike. Oooooh, I know! Maybe they could secretly add it to North Korean Corn Flakes or something.... Anyway, enough of the World's affairs, back to me and my increasingly 'pressing' problem...

My kayaking craze happened around the same time as my sexycise phase. I had become addicted to exercise and to health-foods and was particularly addicted to protein bars. I had read something on the Internet about the benefits of bran. *shakes head* do not believe everything you read on the Internet...... But me being me, I bought a mahoosive consignment of raw bran. Not one for moderation, I started sprinkling it on EVERY-THING! I was gonna be sooooo thin! But then I made a rookie mistake. After my healthy breakfast of bran flakes, with a liberal sprinkling of bran, a bran muffin and a protein and bran shake, feeling sufficiently fortified I went kayaking....

Well...there I was, paddling away to my heart's content, feeling all fit and virtuous, not a care in the world. Well, not until the cramps started. I was far from the shore, all bundled up in my one piece thick snowsuit. (It gets cold on the water, so you have to wrap up warm) Suddenly I had the weirdest feeling in my tummy. Like somebody was plucking on my intestines like guitar strings. At this stage it was only my tummy, so I wasn't TOO concerned. It would pass, no doubt. It would have to, because going for a 'number 2' just wasn't possible in the middle of the bleeding sea. But of course it didn't pass. It started to get worse. Now my sphincter had joined in and 'the dam' was threatening to burst at any moment. I was clenching my buns as hard as I could, but to no avail. I NEEDED to go! End of! There was absolutely no way I could stick me bum over the edge of the kayak. The bleedin thing would topple over if I attempted such a move . And then there was my onesie. There was no way I could get that off. My brain was working overtime desperately trying to find a solution to my terrible dilemma. Just as I was considering the extreme option of slashing the back end of my onesie with my fishin knife, it turned out I no longer had a say in matters... Suddenly a mahooooosive cramp made me double over and simultaneously the floodgates burst ! There really was nothing I could do! I hadn't been in this predicament for nearly fifty years! At least then there was somebody on hand to change me. The force of the sudden and total evacuation almost had the effect of an ejector seat, thrusting me upwards and nearly over the edge of the kayak. My onesie was filled to the brim with recycled bran muffins! Fortunately, the smell was contained and in fairness, the warmth was quite comforting. But the grossness of my predicament hadn't passed me by. On the contrary. What in dog's name was I going to do???? The only saving grace, was that for once, there was nobody to witness my distress. I felt like bursting into tears, but knew it wouldn't help, so I tried to weigh up my options.

1. Paddle for shore, drive home as I am and clean up properly under the shower. This was tempting, but had two possible flaws. I wasn't sure exactly how ..ahem.. 'contained' the situation would remain and didn't want to ming up the car. Even worse, was the possibility of getting caught with my pants down as it were.

2. Paddle for shore, strip off, cleanse self and onesie in ice-cold arctic waters. Run about for a bit to get rid of the worst of the wetness, before driving home and only having to confess to falling in, rather than the significantly more embarrassing truth. This option only had one flaw. That I would die from

hypothermia. It seemed a small price to pay, so this is exactly what I did.

OH LORDY!

7

The Joys of Camping

Camping is a funny old thing, isn't it? I don't mean the pup tent, hiking in the middle of nowhere kind of survival camping. I love that. I am talking about organised camping. Camping in huge equipped tents, on designated campsites. I mean, it's kind of mad if you think about it. Why, when people have a perfectly good and comfortable home, would they not only choose but pay lots of money to camp. To 'make do' in cramped conditions with inferior facilities, sharing with total strangers? Why choose to live like a refugee and pay through the nose for it? It really is quite absurd. If you want to go on holiday, with all the mod cons, book a bleedin hotel for dog's sake. And it's not only the conditions. The whole jolliness of it all is delightfully ironic.

Happy campers greet each other cheerfully.

'Good Morning!' they sing out.

These are the very same people who totally ignore and avoid their lifelong neighbours at home. And as for camping abroad. What is it about the British and their sunbathing idiocy? Maybe it's because we Brits don't see much sun at home? As soon as we arrive at our destination or sometimes already in the departure lounge of our freezing home airports, we strip off. Beer bellies and front bumps bared, we swarm to the beach. It wouldn't be so bad if we knew how to sunbathe, but we don't. Day one, determined to get a sun-kissed face, we lie and bake on our backs all day, not thinking to turn over. The results are catastrophic. Day two sees us unable to walk, lobster red on one side, ghostly pale on the other.

I also have personal reasons for my aversion to camping. Shameful incidents I wish I could forget, but they are tattooed on my consciousness. I still break out in a sweat when I think of them.

He first was on a foreign holiday, the actual location irrelevant. It started in a bar. Lots of drinkies, tequila slammers, the full works. As you no doubt know, evenings involving tequila slammers never end well. Some fellow slammers fared even worse than me and had to get carried out and weren't seen for days. When I was all slammed out, I left the bars (yes, there appeared to be two of them by now) as gracefully as possible. Tripping over invisible obstacles and waving my drunken goodbyes, I felt on top of the world. Until the fresh air hit me. My legs became uncooperative and seemed to work independently of my brain and each other. My internal compass and eyesight had given up the ghost too and heaven knows how long it took me just to get out of the car park. But on I staggered, the terrier in me not about to give up. I scanned the horizon for my bright orange tent. Specially chosen for its ability to stick out like a sore thumb amongst all the other boring greens and blues. And there it was! My beautiful orange dome, a beacon, guiding me homewards to my much-needed bed. After considerable struggling with the zip, I was in. But what was this lump I saw before me? Like a mahoosive caterpillar curled up in its cocoon? I was on my own, not sharing with anybody.

Were my eyes deceiving me? I bent forward to get a closer look, accidentally head banging the poor innocent person, asleep in THEIR sleeping bag, in THEIR orange tent. The combination of shock, humiliation and tequila proved too much for my abused stomach, as I pebble-dashed the crime scene. Yes, to my shame, I puked all over the no longer sleeping and extremely annoyed camper. I ran for my life, desperately seeking my own orange dome, praying that my victim didn't recognise me.

hangs head in shame

I just hope that the person in the unfortunate sleeping bag isn't reading my confession... but if you are, please note, I would take it all back if I could, literally and figuratively.

A second incident, thank dog only a one-nighter, was the following. I suffered from a fear of flying for twenty-three years, which meant travelling everywhere by car. Living above the polar circle and having family in Scotland, meant lots of long car journeys. We didn't have much money, so we spent the nights either in the back of the Land Rover or in a pup tent. This particular night we were at a campsite. We swiftly put up the tent, then had a simple barbecue with a few beers. It was a nice end to a long day's driving. We went to bed early as we wanted to be up at dawn for another long day on the road. The whole journey to Scotland took the best part of a week. Well, you know what beer does to your bladder, don't you? I don't know about you, but when I camp and nature calls in the middle of the night, I don't fumble about getting dressed and shod and making my way to the toilet block. I mean, you would never get back to sleep. Also, in the middle of the night, it's dark and everyone else is asleep. So what's to stop you just opening your tent flap and squatting down in the grass? Nothing, right? So when my bladder woke me, asking to be emptied, still half asleep, I stumbled out of the tent, naked as a mole rat and squatted down in the grass. I was startled out of my trance by voices. Then laughter and cheering. The campers on the pitch next to us were still up! Sitting outside having a drink, just meters away! Now being entertained by the phantom, nudey urinator that was me!

Oh, and then there's the whole toilet and shower thing. Having to traipse for miles to perform your ablutions is such a pain in the arse. But for me, it was more than that, surprise surprise... I actually lived on a campsite I worked on in the South of France for nearly five years, so shower blocks were no stranger to me. Unfortunately for me, it wasn't only people who went there to escape the heat.

One day I was having my shower as usual and while washing my hair I felt something around my ankle. I knew the plugholes sometimes got clogged up by peoples hair. Gross, I know, so I assumed it was some hair that had tangled itself around my leg. I had shampoo in my eyes, so couldn't see, so shook the leg in question vigorously to free it from the unwanted attention. But as I lifted my foot, I suddenly realised that the situation I found myself in was worse. Much worse. I could hardly lift my foot, as whatever was entwined around my ankle was heavy. Very heavy. And it was moving!

OH

MY

DOG!!!!!

As the soap cleared out of my eyes I managed to look down and saw what was constricting me.... IT WAS ONLY A FRICKIN SNAKE!!!!!!! Screaming like a girlie I streaked out of the cubicle, dragging my serpentined leg behind me!

'Hellllllllllllp', I cried, caring not a jot that I was in me bleedin' birthday suit.

Luckily I didn't have to wait long for rescue. The campsite gardener was on hand and calmly de-snaked me. I just prayed he didn't recognise me without my clothes on, but I avoided him for the rest of the season just in case. It was probably only a grass snake or something, but I can assure you I didn't linger when showering after that!

OH LORDY!

8

Murder on Their Mind

Hill walking is my favourite thing. Hill walking with my dogs, my idea of heaven. Apart from one thing, ironically enough, something that would get me a one-way ticket there. When hiking, my dogs try to kill me. I only have one dog now, a border terrier called Pønky. My other lovely old boy went to the Bridge last year. I miss him intensely. I talk of him here in the present tense, as I still feel him with me. I don't know if you have dogs, or if any of this sounds familiar. I would hate to think it was something personal and that my dogs have some kind of a vendetta to kill me. Border terriers are otherwise fantastic dogs. They are incredible characters - feisty, cheeky, naughty and very loving. They have strong individual personalities. My two are total and utter opposites in every way. Every way, bar one. Their murderous intentions towards me. Their intentions identical, their attempts at achieving their goal, completely different. As I said, I hope it is 'just a dog or border terrier thing', but if not, I suspect I know why they are trying to kill me....

It may well find its roots in an early expedition I took them on, many years ago. I chose a hill I wanted to climb. As you know I detest instructions, so refused to even consult a map, to see if there was an advised route, or path up said hill. I just set off. Surely the logical manner of ascent would become apparent....

I discovered what looked to be a path, sneaking up between the pine trees. It soon became apparent that I was wrong, it was just an animal track. The trees became denser, the ascent steeper. B*gger. Well, I refused to turn back, so we soldiered on. The dogs weren't bothered at this stage because they still had plenty room beneath the branches. I, on the other hand, was getting scratched to bits and had to resort to climbing backwards through the branches so I wouldn't lose an eye. Of course, the dogs were on leads and started to get tangled up and annoyed. Not as annoyed as me though, as I had to keep untangling them. But I wasn't going to let any of this stop me. Oh no. Eventually, we got above the tree line and I scanned the hillside looking for a way up. It was waaay too steep to go straight up, so we zigzagged over the uneven ground. It was exhausting, physically and mentally. My arms were aching too from holding on to the dogs' leads, so tightly as one misstep could be fatal. As we got higher still, our options were restricted. To our left was a huge area of scree, impossible to walk on without causing a landslide, to our right a thick and impenetrable high gorse. The only way up was straight up. And it was steep, very, very steep. I could no longer walk upright, so the three of us were on all fours. Both dogs were becoming increasingly nervous and reluctant. And who could blame them? I could SEE them thinking ' where the hell are you taking us'. I was having to coax them now, but they had lost faith in me completely. Simultaneously, they stopped in their tracks. They simply refused to go further, knowing instinctively it would mean their certain deaths.

'Ok then, have it your own way', I muttered sarcastically to my mutineers.

'You win, we'll go back down'.

But turning around, it became obvious that this was not going to be easy. It was a sheer slope, vertigo-inducing. Not only would the dogs not go up, they also refused to go DOWN! They were rooted to the spot, quivering and whining. What on earth was I going to do now?

There really was only one thing I could do. I grabbed one dog under each arm and slid down the slope on my bum! Over sticking out rocks and gorse, down we went. Fortunately, they both kept still, probably still frozen by fear. On we slid, my arse now red raw and quite possibly bleeding, we landed back at the tree line. I didn't dare let them off their leads, as slipping would still have been treacherous. So we wrestled our way back down through the tightly knitted, cruel and sharp pine trees. I was constantly having to untangle the poor sods. At last, we got through and back onto normal terrain. I still couldn't let them off lead as they would have run from their mad owner and never come back. I swear when I went to take them out for their evening pee that day they both ran and hid from me, terrified that I would take them climbing again.

So, ever since that day, I reckon they have been plotting my demise and this is how they go about it. Jacky is a gentle giant. Walking uphill, he is a stoic plodder, quite possibly his way of lulling me into a false sense of security? Going down, however, is a different matter entirely. Whether due to his momentum, being a big boy or his evil intentions, he trots downhill like a young 'un., gaining speed all the time. As he is on lead, I have no choice but to follow... more often than not at neck-breaking speeds. Not having time to secure my footing, he will suddenly screech to a halt right in front of me, as he has an urgent need to poop; or lick his boy parts; or some other fabrication of his.

This causes me to lose my balance and my footing. I trip over him, my fate, in his paws. Sometimes I just land on my arse, from which I can bounce back up, sometimes somersaulting out of control towards a cliff face. Another method of his, he uses in the winter months, is leading me over snowfields he knows will take his weight, but not mine. He walks 'innocently' over a frozen lake, as I plunge through to my icy death.

Jacky loves his food. Well, he loves ANYBODY's food if he gets the chance. He is a big boy and a big eater. What goes in must come out. Fact. That too is his trusted method of attempting murder. Murder by methane poisoning. That or snogging me to death with his rotten fish breath.

Pønky's methods are even more sneaky. She is a born hunter, a killer actually, a murderin' b*tch. She sees a hill walk purely as an opportunity to kill things. Unfortunately for me, I am top of her list. She either opts for a sudden lunge at something, only seen by her, jerking me off balance and teetering into a canyon or startling a rock ptarmigan or other animal, which flurries squawkingly away, causing me a cardiac event. Have you ever startled one of these birds? The sound they make is terrifying, like a bleedin massacre.

Another tactic of hers is a dogfight. Fortunately, we hardly ever meet other dogs, as we live in the middle of nowhere, but if we do, it never ends well. Usually for me. Pønky hates other dogs, in fact, she hates everything. She does not discriminate. If an unleashed dog approaches her, she will try and rip its throat out. I am the poor victim as I come between the two trying to avoid bloodshed. But the little b*tch always ends up biting me! She is constantly on the lookout for animals or birds when she sees one she will go in for the chase, normally after sheep, trailing me behind her bleeding out, my skin in tatters. Oh, and recently she has thought up an ingenious method. She deliberately shakes her dander out all over me, as she KNOWS I have a dog allergy. It sends me into mucusy fits of coughing and sneezing, one of which may just carry me off one of these days. They are both evil, but I love them to bits and wouldn't change a thing...OH LORDY!

Murderin' Mutts

9

Beachcombing

Just because I used to frequent nudey beaches, that does not make me a nudist. No. I don't go flashin my bits about, nor perving at others. Honest Guv. However, when I used to work in the South of France many moons ago, the nudist beaches were the only quiet ones and with hardly any children. So when we had some well deserved time off, we went there. But again, no flashing, nor perving. Just lazing in the sun.

One fine day, while basking on the sand, I decided to cool off a bit by going snorkelling. There is a lot to see in the Mediterranean, even just with a snorkel, quite close to the shore. So in I went. Snorkelling innocently away, I suddenly felt something flapping against my face! Peeking tentatively through my diving mask, I clocked something brown and dangly! Oh, my dog nooooo!!!! I felt defiled. Dirty. It could only be one thing here in the sea on the nudey beach.....a man's errant dangler!!!! I was mortified and thought he may be too, as surely such an act couldn't be deliberate? So I didn't surface straight away, swam on as if nothing had happened. I flippered to the shore, left the water without looking at my fellow ahem 'swimmer' and plonked myself back down on my towel. I swapped my mask for my sunglasses and surreptitiously eyeballed my assailant. There was only one man in the proximity, still waist deep in the water. That must be him. Now he too started making his way to the shore. I grabbed a book to hide behind, while sneakily watching him surface and come out of the sea. My mouth dropped open. I couldn't believe my eyes. No, not because of his dangler, naughty readers, although it was there too. But it was shadowed into insignificance by a mahoooosive catheter he had hanging around his waist not a pee pee one, one full of an extended family of otters. So it wasn't 'junior' that slapped me in the face, it was his flapping sack of smelly poop!!!!! **No disrespect to people with colostomy bags, I just don't think they shud go flappin them about in peoples faces...I mean, I dont go stickin my bum in theirs now do I?

OH LORDY!

People are drawn to the beach for all manner of reasons. You have the sunbathers, the rock poolers, the dog walkers, the fishermen. Me, I am a beachcomber. Just love driftwood and all the other treasures you can find on the beach. It's also a great place to find skulls, which I collect. Once upon a time, when I had a holiday home on the East coast of Scotland, I found an awesome seal skull. I say skull, I actually mean head, Well, in truth, it was still attached to the body, but it WAS dead, so don't be too horrified. I realised I couldn't carry the whole seal back with me, coz that would have been gross, right? So, I went about lightening the load. I didn't have any cutting tools with me, so made do with what was readily available in the vicinity in the way of sticks and stones. I will spare you the grizzly details, suffice to say, I got my trophy and carried my trophy home. Once I got home, I wasn't entirely sure how to deal with my smelly friend and it had started raining, so I just left it outside in a bucket, intending to deal with it later. But of course, I forgot all about it. The holiday ended and I had to return to Holland to work and it was a couple of months before I returned. I was greeted by the most horrific smell ever. It smelled like a rotten seal head in a bucket of rainwater, which was exactly what it was. Oops. Then I remembered how I had casually dumped and abandoned my poor little seal friend in its watery grave. I felt so guilty. I approached the bucket, gagging and retching. 'I must save my seal and return his dignity! I will clean his skull to proudly display and give his remains a Christian burial', I vowed. But, how? I could hardly dip my hands in....So, I decided to pour out the contents of the reeking bucket over the outside drain. My frayed logic deducted that this would cause the rainwater to drain away, leaving the seal head on the grate. What I hadn't accounted for, however, was here, months of decomposition. Oh, my good dog! I started pouring, but instead of the rainwater I expected, it was gloop, thick chunky gloop. The smell was all-encompassing. Even though I held my free hand over my mouth and nose, it permeated everything. I could feel it entering me through my very pores. I continued pouring the primordial soup, but where was my treasure? The bucket was now empty, yet it was nowhere to be seen. How on earth was that possible? It must have decomposed completely, skull and all. I took the grate off the drain so the slimy chunks would also disappear. But they didn't. Ooops. I had only gone and blocked the drain! The disintegrated skull, together with the seal fat had clogged up the sewage pipe. I tried everything - poking at it with sticks, bombarding it with rocks, flooding it, but no. I had no choice but to call the council. As I had no neighbours to blame, I was going to have to come clean and this meant paying for their services, which made the tightwad in me cry. They arrived in due course, with their rods and special equipment. I had managed to get rid of the worst of the smell by now, with lashings of disinfectant and washing up liquid.

Drain unblocking bloke- (in broad Scottish brogue) 'So, whit happund here, hen? Ye didnae go flushin yer fanny pads doon the bog, did ya?

Me (feigning outrage)- 'Certainly not !!!! It's body parts!'

The poor bloke look horrified. He wasn't sure how to proceed and whether he would be deemed an accomplice for helping me to get rid of evidence of a murder. I tried to pacify him by explaining that it was 'only an animal' I was trying to dispose of. Now, instead of being ready to call the Police, he looked like he was about to call a Shrink and get me committed!

OH LORDY!

There is only one thing I truly regret in life and that is handing over my absolute best and unique beach find to the Police. 'How did this come about?' you wonder...

Well.... it was years ago now, before Pønky (some people use AD or BC or other such things to mark time, I use BP- before Pønky and BJ.) Noooo, not that !!!! Get your mind out of the gutter- BJ =before Jacky. This story takes place BP, so it was me, Willem and the handsome Jacky, walking on the picturesque Elie beach in Scotland. As per usual, we were playing ball. Reaching down to pick up one of the balls, we literally stumbled upon something quite remarkable.

'Oh my dog, it's a dick!', cried Willem.

Like myself, he is rather prone to flights of fancy, so my immediate reaction was an eye roll. Also, we love arguing, sometimes deliberately disagreeing with each other, him because he is contrary, me because I am always right. So, on gazing down upon the phallus-like object, I begged to differ.

'That ain't no dick', I retorted. 'How could it be? What would a lone knob be doing washed up on the beach?'

But Willem insisted.

'Trust me, I'm a man and I know a dangler when I see one!'

Both of us were now entranced by the appendage, lying lost and forlorn amongst the seaweed. It was black and necrotic looking. Well, what do you expect? It would hardly be at its best, separated from its owner and its blood supply in particular. We grabbed a nearby stick and started prodding at it, in case it was a dog turd, or something else cunningly disguised as a Pinkus. I stabbed at its fireman's helmet, poking it downwards. Totally aghast, I watched, as it slipped down, revealing a pink tumescent shaft underneath! I am not entirely sure if tumescent is the right word, but I simply love it, (the word that is. Obviously) and have been dying to use it. Well, surely it couldn't be a dog turd then? I mean, have YOU ever seen a dog turd with a foreskin? No, me neither.... So now, we were thoroughly convinced that our find was indeed a human penis! OH.....MY....DOG !!!! I flipped it over with the stick. Yes, the stick. I may be gross, but even I wasn't planning on touching it with my bare hands. For starters, I didn't want to have my fingerprints all over it. I mean, imagine if it turned out to be a murder and I got the blame! Upside down now, it looked even more horrific. Not only was it a schlong, it had a bleedin ball sack! Bag of marbles! It looked like it had been cut off by a scalpel, so clean cut was the edge. My imagination now started working overtime. I was enchanted. I felt its pain. It's one shrivelled eye, looked up at me, pleadingly. How on earth could this have happened? I reckoned it was a jealous wife who found her hubby in bed with her best friend and sliced it off in a fit of rage. Willem of course disagreed. Par for the course. He thought it may be 'medical waste' I countered that a surplus swizzer would surely be incinerated? Sticking to my theory, this dismemberment- DIS MEMBER MENT * sniggers * would surely mean murder. You don't get your todger sliced off and live to tell the tale, do you? At this point, we also noticed that under its bed of seaweed, lay a considerable amount of plastic sheeting. Could the rest of the poor chap be buried underneath? I started digging with my foot.

'No' cried, Willem, 'we have to call the Police. We could be tampering with evidence...this could be a crime scene.'

Feeling slightly guilty at my totally inappropriate glee, I announced in a deep, official voice..

'You stay here with Jacky and guard the prick... there is a pub just up there, I will go and call the cops'

So off I ran to the nearby pub, hardly able to contain my excitement at getting caught up in something so C.S.I- like. The phone was situated at the end of the bar. I grabbed it and dialled.

Me -'erm hello, good morning. I am phoning to report a possible crime.'

Cops - 'go on'

Me- 'well, we have just found some body parts on the beach in Elie'

Cops- 'body parts? What kind of body parts?

Me-(in hushed voice, coz bar full of customers) ' man's ahem... 'toolbox'

Cops- I beg your pardon, ma'am? A toolbox is not body parts. Maybe there is a workman in the area.

Me- 'Nooooo, you don't understand! I have found a man's

penis!

Everyone in the bar turned to look at me as if I had escaped from the local loony bin.

Cops- *shocked silence* A penis? Are you sure?

Me- Of course, I am sure! I know a bleedin penis when I see one!

Cops- 'it's bleeding?'

Me- 'Nooooo. Do try and understand... it's dead... deceased.. dismembered.

Cops- 'Ok, we are on our way'

I could hear them thinking, 'crank', but content that I had done my civic duty, I returned to the scene of the crime. We waited, unsure if the Police would actually turn up. In the meantime, of course, we fabricated every possible scenario. As the minutes passed, our 'explanations' became wilder and wilder. And of course, me being me, I immediately imagined there being a 'finders fee', not that the owner would be around to claim his 'baby maker', but maybe a reward from the Police for helping solve a crime! Yayayyayy. A police car turned up and two local 'Bobbies' stepped out. They walked towards us, one with a shovel over his shoulder. It looked very comical, very Laurel and Hardy. I started giggling, which probably didn't give the best impression. The policemen glared at me, probably still thinking it was a hoax. Willem took charge and showed them our find. Their demeanour changed. They both looked uncomfortable, flinching and crossing their legs as if in pain.

'It IS a penis!', they cried.

They immediately separated us and started interviewing us. Oh, my dog ! Were we SUSPECTS???? Surely not...I just prayed our stories would corroborate, as I hadn't accounted for this happening. I concentrated on looking innocent. The young officer was obviously embarrassed asking me questions about 'junior'. The questions over, the tension relieved, the policemen also started laughing and joking as they put John Thomas into a wee baggy.

'Well, that's that then', they said and made to leave. I felt cheated.

Me – 'Wait a minute. You can't just go. Do you not need to put crime tape up? Secure the scene?'

Cops – 'Erm... no...'

Me – 'But what about the plastic sheeting? There may be more of him'

Cops–(condescendingly) 'You watch too much television. There was a 'jumper' off the Forth Road bridge a couple of days ago. This will be his...'

And off they went. I was flabbergasted. They couldn't know that for sure. And you don't get a clean cut like that from anything but a scalpel. Maybe they were just rookies, or just pure lazy, couldn't be bothered with the extra work and paperwork involved. I don't know. What I do know, is that I regretted handing over my phallic trophy. It would have looked lovely on my mantelpiece......

OH LORDY!

The Necrotic Knob

Although the necrotic knob was surely my best find, the crème de la crème if you like, there have been some other good 'uns through the years. I had become so fond of beachcombing, that Willem bought me the perfect gift for my fortieth birthday- a metal detector! I was so excited when I unwrapped it and saw what it was. I had always wanted one, had envisioned myself unearthing hidden treasures from times gone by, Viking helmets, swords and daggers from battles past and of course golden coins and lots of 'em. I was gonna be RICH! But, like most of my hopes and dreams, it just wasn't to be. Willem packed me and Jacky and the shiny new metal detector into his rigid inflatable dinghy, revved up the engine and off we set. He was taking us to an uninhabited island, off the coast of Holland, in the North Sea. I was sooo happy. It was my birthday. I had everything I wanted. My big handsome dog Jacky, my lovely, generous husband and of course the new love of my life – my metal detector! I couldn't believe my luck.... We had now left the calm waters of the harbour and had hit the open sea. Choppy doesn't come close. The waves were huge. But I had faith in captain Willem, who capably chartered a course between the waves. I caught a glimpse of my treasure island, on the horizon, I gleefully shouted...

'Land Ahoy!'

Jacky too was smiling, his long flowing beard blowing in the wind. Suddenly, out of nowhere, we were hit by a mahooosive wave and I watched as my precious fortune finder was launched in the air, like a rocket bound for space. My mouth fell open, my hands reached out. But to no avail. My beautiful metal detector landed in the sea and with a huge splash, it promptly sank. Willem hadn't tied my precious down! My dreams were shattered, my newfound love lost. All I could do now was hope it would wash up somewhere, someday. Then we would be reunited....and I could whack Willem round the head with it.

I didn't let the loss get to me, however and I continued scouring the beaches with zest. Not once, but twice, I found something that I was convinced would be my salvation. My luck had turned. I didn't need a metal detector. I would find my own fortune. Looking back now, I feel suitably ridiculous...

The first was on a beach that was new to me. Combing along, my eye was drawn to a glint up ahead. The sun was catching on something and it was big and shiny. As always, when spotting something interesting, my heartbeat picked up and my imagination started working overtime. It was an almost hexagonal shape, large like a rock and shiny like a jewel. I became convinced it was a crystal, or quite possibly even a diamond! Yes, a rough diamond, that is what it was! I picked it up and lugged it all the way back to the car, my hands nearly falling off because of the awkward shape. Even if they had, it would not have stopped me, oh no. I would have soldiered on, clasping my treasure between bloodied stumps, so convinced I was of it's worth. But what to do with it now? I decided to put it outside in the garden for now, just in case it was dangerous. Radioactive? Explosive? Combustible? You can't be too careful... I scoured the yellow pages to find someone who could identify, value and hopefully buy I from me. I found a number for a precious stone seller, vowed to phone him in the morning, a took myself smugly off to bed. I was woken by the pattering of rain on the window, checked the time to see if I could phone already and went outside to collect my 'diamond'. My precious stone, was now considerably smaller than it was yesterday and surrounded by what looked like smaller crystals. I reached out and touched its surface, causing more crystals to fall off. Then it hit me.... My huge valuable diamond was not a diamond after all! Not even a quartz, or some other less precious stone. It was a bleedin' salt cube!!!!! You know? The things farmers put in their fields to satisfy the herds' natural craving for salt, so they don't go gnawing on trees or rocks. Thank dog I had discovered the truth BEFORE I turned up with it at the jewel expert! I mean can you imagine?????

Learning from my mistakes is not on of my strong points. This is made apparent by my other 'valuable discovery' years later. I put it down to enthusiasm.... I do tend to get carried away by it.... I had been reading in the paper about a man who had been out walking his dog on a beach in Wales and stumbled across a large piece of ambergris. He went on to sell it for twenty thousand pounds! Do you know ambergris? It's bleedin whale vomit or something. Absolutely gross, but it contains some property that sustains odour. It is used by perfume makers to make their smellies stay smelly if you get my drift. Totally ironic and weird, coz the stuff stinks to high heaven. Well, it would, wouldn't it? Anyway, in the newspaper article, there was a photo of the fortunate man, holding aloft his whiffy find. It looked like a cross between a piece of sandstone and a huge turd! Of course, having seen this, I couldn't resist a trip to the beach. After all, if he could find it, why not me? I walked for miles and miles, not doing my usual scanning for any old thing, but with a fixed image in my mind. I was looking for ambergris, whale vomit, the more the merrier! My legs were getting tired, my eyes too and just as I was ready to throw in the towel, I caught a terrible whiff. A smell so strong, you could almost hear it. A mixture of death, decay, bodily fluids and rotten fish. Then there it was! A whopping great lump of ambergris! Something as pungent as that couldn't be anything else could it? And it looked EXACTLY like the photo in the paper.

'Wooooofhoooooo', I yelled out... 'Quids in!'

I grabbed it and chucked it in my rucksack. Who cares if the smell ruined the rucksack? I could always buy a new one. I could buy a THOUSAND new ones!!!! I had a quick scour in the vicinity in case the whale had been a bulimic and there were more lumps of it's puke washed up, but no. I wasn't disappointed, though. It just made my actual find more special. I skipped all the way back home and immediately browsed the Net to find out what to do next. I soon found an address of a laboratory who tested the stuff and one for a perfume factory who bought it. I couldn't believe it was so easy! So I sealed my lovely whale vomit in a jiffy bag and sent it off. A week later, a letter arrived from the lab. I was quivering with excitement, wondering how much my puke was worth!!! Well, remember I told you ambergris looked a bit like a cross between a piece of sandstone and a turd? Erm, the lab had tested my ambergris and found it to be EXACTLY that!!!! It was a piece of sandstone that a dog, or fox or something had crapped on and it had merged together into a stinking mass of something that wasn't worth shit!

OH LORDY!

And then there was the whelk debacle *rolls eyes* Yet another total embarrassment. Shortly after having run away from university due to my 'pregnancy', I needed to find a way to make some money. While walking on the beach one day, I spotted some people gathering things out of the rock pools. They had buckets with them and were hard at work. I approached them and asked them what they were doing. They explained they were collecting whelks, left in the rocks on the outgoing tide and that they sold them to a local fishmonger. My heart skipped a beat. How absolutely perfect. There were millions of whelks all over this stretch of rocky coastline, just waiting to be plucked by me and transformed into gold. I rushed off to kit myself out as a professional whelk hunter/gatherer. I procured the following: a tide table, an alarm clock, a small bucket for gathering, a huge barrel for emptying and keeping whelks alive in, a pair of wellies and a large dose of determination. Every day for a week, I lived by the tides. I was having to get up at four am in the half dark. I would work for hours in the cold and wet, slipping and stumbling over seaweedy rocks, but knowing that every time I scored a handful of whelks it meant money! It was hard work, bending and carrying, but I was so good at it! My greed kept me focussed. I grabbed and snatched, grabbed and snatched, filling bucket after bucket. I never missed a tide, was out in all weathers. Finally, my barrel was full and off to the fishmongers, I went. It was time to reap the benefits of my hard labour. Lugging my barrel inside, I was met by a stony glare.

Fishmonger- 'what have you got there hen?'

Me-(trying to sound professional) 'Whelks! And plenty of 'em!

Him-(sarcastically) 'Aye? Let's be seeing them, then.'

Me-(proudly displaying wares) 'Tadaaaaaa!!!!'

Him- (niggering condescendingly) ' Call them whelks? They are no bloody good to anybody, they are far too small .'

At this point, he produced a mesh griddle and scooped a handful of my unworthy whelks up, throwing them on the top. They all fell through, rattling accusingly. Apparently, real whelk pickers use one of these griddles to separate the sellable ones from the bleedin miniature baby midget pygmy primordial dwarves that I had a whole barrel of. He looked at me with disgust, like

I was an idiot of the first order and a baby killer to boot. The realisation sunk in ...I was a whelk nonce! These were just babies! With as much dignity as I could muster, I grabbed the barrel and ran away. Trying to redeem myself, I poured my poor baby whelks back into the sea, hoping I hadn't traumatised them too much.

OH LORDY!

10

Jack of all Trades, Master of None

Once free from the shackles of owing money, I went on to have many different jobs, with varying degrees of success and bedlam. Winging it has always been one of my favourite things and is a great recipe for disaster. But you don't want to hear about success, surely? In this chapter, I will share with you some of my epic job fails. I love variation and change, so have done a bit of everything through the years - babysitting, cleaning, home help, holiday repping, travel guiding, tutoring, teaching, counselling, working with teenage tearaways, handicapped people, autistic people, to name but a few. At the moment, I am working for myself as a yarn artist, (a term I made up by the way) I make mainly dogs and other animals, also for dog charities and the like. I love working, but find it extremely cruel and inhumane that normal employment does not allow for afternoon naps. It's a travesty! Having had lots of different jobs, there have been many ..ahem.. incidents. Here are a few of them, who knows there may be a sequel ... .Ok, enough of an intro, let's get down to the dirty details.

Incident 1 - The Babysittin Balls Up

When I first moved to Holland in my early twenties, I didn't speak the language well enough to get a 'proper' job, so I started out babysitting to help learn the language and make a bit of money. I have a strong maternal instinct. Unfortunately, directed only towards four legged fur babies - namely cats and dogs. Of human babies and young children, I know nothing at all....But babysit I did. On one particular occasion, I was looking after a very young child. I can't remember how old, just that it couldn't talk. They were my favourite kind, the ones that couldn't tell tales of my incompetence to mummy and daddy. Well, off the parents went and I was left with my charge. They would be gone all day, so I wanted to do a variety of things, so I, I mean 'it' wouldn't get bored. It was a sunny day, so I decided to take it to the play park. We got there, all smiles and had the place to ourselves. (which turned out to be a blessing, as there would be no witnesses)

'So?,' I said to the child, 'What do you want to play on?'

It looked at me blankly, probably coz it couldn't talk?

'No preference, eh? Ok, I'll decide for you. Let's go on the swings'.

They were always my favourite. So, I lifted it out of its pram and put it on the swing. This is where me ignorance probably started to show. A child, so young it could not talk, may also not be able to hold on very well? Indeed, this turned out to be the case.... It sat happily enough on the swing. It even started sucking its thumb, which also should probably have alerted me that things weren't as they should be. But I was enthusiastic. We were going to have FUN! So I gave the swing an almighty push, cheering encouragingly, only to see the toddler soar up into the sky, catapulted off the swing, into the blue yonder. It lets out a piercing scream, which turned into a chilling yowl, as it landed on its face, on what I hoped wasn't too hard concrete. Whoops !!! My maternal instinct wasn't working too well that day, because I remember my first thought being ' I hope there won't be any visible damage', rather than 'I hope it's ok'. Yes, I probably should also have known it's actual gender, but nobody is perfect... I rushed over to assess the damage. My luck was not in. Like in a cartoon, you could actually see the bump develop on its forehead! It was huge! Shit, what to do???? First, I needed it to shut up, as the last thing I needed was spectators, so I plonked it back in its carriage and raced it off to a nearby ice cream van, where I tried desperately to placate it with a 99 cone. I THINK it was old enough to eat solids???? Didn't want to add choking to my misdemeanours. Oh well, there ain't a great difference between a ladies front bump and an ice cream cone and it seemed to do the trick. I held an ice lolly to the bump, hoping in vain, it would go down. At least it wasn't showing signs of brain damage, not that I am sure what they would be. So, it all came down to culpability. I needed to divert the blame away from me. This wasn't an easy task, considering I was the one who was supposed to be in charge. But, this was my field of expertise. I had years of experience in this, my poor brother often taking the blame and punishment for my naughtiness. I could hardly blame the kid itself. That didn't seem fair, as it was so young and again, that I was supposed to be looking after it. I wracked my brains and came up with a foolproof plan...

I rushed back home, not forgetting the little one, who was now also covered in 'this will make you better' flavoured ice cream. I stuck it in front of sesame street with a bag of frozen peas on its head and set about rewriting history... I collected the mother's shoes, from their neat and tidy resting place in the hall and deposited them just in front of the coffee table, that had delightfully pointy corners. Genius! So when the parents returned, I had the perfect explanation for the bump on the forehead. The poor mite had tripped over NAUGHTY mummy's shoes, that SHE had discarded like deathly traps in the living room.

OH LORDY!

Incident 2 – the Belgian Chocolates

I am not a great one for housework. Don't get me wrong, I am not a Minger. Well, not a total Minger. I believe in hygiene, clean the toilet once a week, that kind of thing. But my attempts at cleaning are very much hit and miss and when the urge takes me. I also never clean anything above eye level, coz what you don't see can't hurt you *nods* But I do love to Hoover. Hoovering makes me feel virtuous.

When I first moved to Holland in my early twenties, I needed a job. Not speaking the language yet, cleaning was one job I could get and learn the language at the same time. Rumour has it, in my first job, cleaning offices, I broke the central heating system. Allegedly, when cleaning the windows instead of going to get a ladder, I just stood on the wall radiator, causing it to snap off and spill water everywhere. No comment. I decided that home helping was maybe more my thing.....

I had a selection of oldies to visit and help with whatever they needed. Some were really nice and grateful. Some were nasty and bitter. But none more so than Mrs Candle. Yes, that really was her name. Let me describe her to you. She was old and stooped, but could still walk. She didn't wear clothes, but had a shawl wrapped around her wizened frame. Her steely gray long hair was scruffily tied up in a greasy bun. She had been a children's writer when she was younger. Dog knows what the books were about. She could easily be cast in one of them as a witch, all she lacked was a cauldron. She lived in a big house, yet used only one room. I think it had been the living room, but now housed a bed. Everything was absolutely filthy. It turned out that it hadn't been cleaned in years. Mrs Candle would not allow it. The curtains were kept closed all the time, the floor was covered in newspaper, rather than carpet. Layer upon layer of it. The bed was just a bare, stained mattress with a grubby blanket. No sheets, no nothing. The gas fire in the room was on full all the time. I swear it must have been 35 degrees Celsius inside. ' So why was I there?' you are no doubt wondering if I wasn't allowed to clean. I had two tasks. One was to feed the Witch. The second – you may want to skip this bit if you are of a fragile disposition..... was to empty her commode chair. This would be bad enough under normal circumstances, but here the circumstances were anything BUT normal. There was a vicious circle at play. A VERY, VERY smelly, sickening one......

Her kitchen was a total health hazard. There were grease and dirt everywhere, flies buzzing about, even mouse or rat droppings in the corner. As for the fridge, it was blue with mould, absolutely disgusting. The Witch would only eat one thing and it was my job to make it – mashed up potatoes and mashed up cauliflower. ' Whatever floats your boat', I thought as I went about my task of making it. I drained the cooked food and reached into the fridge for some butter to mash it up with. To my horror, I saw that the butter was totally rancid. I felt it my duty to tell the Witch and did just that. I asked her if she wanted me to go buy some new butter, but she crowed back...

'That's just the way I like it!'

So rancid butter it was. She slobbered it all up, wiped her mouth with her shawl and then plonked herself down on the commode. Oh dear. Oh, dearie dear. Suffice to say, SHE might like her butter rancid, but her bleedin guts most certainly didn't.

Once the steam had lifted I went about my second job. The emptying of the commode. The silly Witch could walk perfectly well, so could have used the toilet. I am sure she did this just for the fun of it. But I wasn't going to let her see that it bothered me. Just took one mahoooosive breath in, lifted the warm bucket and poured it down the toilet, only drawing breath after having flushed with one hand and wildly sprayed air freshener with the other. The cycle continued day after day. Rancid butter and commode. I knew I couldn't change the stubborn witch, so just dealt with it as best I could. I just had one vow. While in her house I would never, NEVER eat or drink anything myself. At least this way, I wouldn't get ill. But one day, one sorry, SORRY day, I forgot. I had only just arrived, so was caught with my guard down. As I walked into the overheated stinking living room, the crone reached out to me. She was proffering a box of Belgian chocolates, with a smile on her face. I had never seen her smile before, so I may have been transfixed or even enchanted.

'Here my child, take one'

In hindsight, it would not have been a smile at all, but an evil sadistic grin. I stupidly took a chocolate and put it in my mouth. Just as I was swallowing, the old crone laid the box back down on the floor, RIGHT IN FRONT OF HER FRICKIN COMMODE!!!! IN THE DRIP ZONE!!!

OH LORDY

Incident 3.

Most of my jobs have revolved around me looking after people. Ironic, really, as I can hardly look after MYSELF properly. One of my favourite jobs, was as an activity care worker, in a small village for handicapped people. It was a fantastic place, with group and individual residences, shop, restaurant, café, sports hall and activity centre, kind of like a University campus. I loved thinking up fun things to do and doing them with my 'charges'. I didn't always do my homework well, however and failed to read up on medical notes and the like, preferring the 'hands-on' approach... You know me, I hate instruction manuals and being told what to do. How hard could it be?

I was allocated a lovely young lad, called Simon. He was about seventeen and was autistic. He was an enthusiastic chap and crazy about driving. He wasn't able to actually learn to drive but was obsessed by it. So, I thought I would be doing him a favour by taking him out to the beach where they had go-karts. We had a whale of a time. Well, to start off with....How was I supposed to know he had some kind of swallowing problem???? Ok, ok, it MAY have been in his notes. That's right...rub it in. It may have been in his notes that 'eating must be supervised closely at all times' blah blah blah... I thought I was being nice treating him to an ice cream. How was I to know he would nearly choke to death on the bleeding thing. But don't worry. He is fine. I coolly performed the Heimlich manoeuvre and swore him to secrecy.

To assure he would keep his promise, I thought it best to distract him with another activity that would take his mind off his near death experience. Back at the campus, they had special bikes, called side by sides. I don't know if you know them? They are like trikes and have two seats (real seats, not saddles) and two sets of handlebars and pedals next to each other. The only difference between the two sides is one side is meant for the 'driver', the other for the passenger. The driver's side has the brakes and controls the steering. As you can guess, it's supposed to be the one in charge (me) that sits in the driver's seat. However, I was buying Simon's silence, so I let him sit on the driver's side. Rookie mistake. He was a big strapping lad and with both of us pedalling and whooping with joy (him pretending to be a taxi driver), we were soon whizzing along at the speed of light. So fast, that I noticed too late, that we were heading straight for the activity centre. Straight for the double glass doors of the activity centre to be precise. The doors were automatic and open once they register a person or a wheelchair wanting to get through. We, however, were approaching said doors at a squillion miles an hour.

I screamed, 'Stop Simon, stop!!!!'

But to no avail. Simon was in his element and deaf to my cries of despair.

'Yeeeeeeeeeeeeeeeeeeeeehaaaaaaaaaaaw !!!!!!!', he cater-wauled

I was powerless. He commanded both the steering wheel and the brakes, yet had no intention of using either.

Luckily there was nobody behind the doors because we crashed straight through them in a shower of glass. This broke Simon out of his joyful reverie, thank dog and he managed to brake just in time as the director came out of his office and fired me on the spot.

OH LORDY

11

Home Surgery

Some people have called me 'ginger' before. *mutters to self * May they rest in peace....I am not ginger. No. I wish I was. I am a boring mouse colour, possibly with a reddish hue if the light shines on it. I do, however confess to the ginger skin. You know, that translucent slug-like pale blue that takes a week to get white. And freckles...freckles everywhere. Not only the small ones, also those horrid big moley ones that I choose to call beauty spots. Not the REALLY gross black hairy ones, but bad enough. I look like I have been splatted by 'dire rear'. Anyway, sorry to bore you with the skin/hair thing, but I promise it's relevant.

Having worked in the South of France for five years, I have done a fair bit of sunbathing, way too much for my fair Scottish skin. I had noticed for a while that my moles were multiplying and not only was I getting more of them, they were also getting bigger. Not only that, they were changing shape and colour. I remembered having read somewhere that this was not a good thing. One mole on my tummy was particularly worrying. It had gained the size of a two pence piece with a hideous raised black centre. It was at this point, that I made the fatal mistake....I consulted 'Dr Google'! I really must warn you, whatever is wrong with you, however worrying, never, EVER google your symptoms. You WILL die. Fact. Sneezing and tickly cough? A common cold, allergies perhaps? Purleeeeeze! Dr Google diagnoses the Zika virus (keep warm until death). A stiff neck and headache? Flu, or maybe a pulled muscle? Wrong again! Dr Google diagnoses meningitis with a side of lockjaw. Readers, friends, please take heed. If you are under the weather, feeling ill at all, just stay away from the computer and all will be well.

You can no doubt guess MY diagnosis.... Not only skin cancer, but the very worst kind, melanoma. The photos of the diseased and deadly moles looked just like mine. Any normal person would have gone straight to the doctor, but not me. For three very good reasons..

1. I had lost all faith in the medical mafia because of my Appendicitis cock-up.

2. I had had the moles for such a long time I was convinced it was too late anyway.

3. I was TERRIFIED.

So, I came up with a sensible solution of my own. I would drink. I would drink enough to stop worrying, enough even to forget what it was I was worried about. Genius. Strangely enough, my plan didn't work. So, one night after a couple of bottles of wine, I decided I had had enough. I would bite the bullet. Who says I need a doctor to rid me of my affliction. I would do it myself. Yes !!! Home surgery was the answer. Unfortunately the excessive drinking was causing me to have delusions of grandeur. *enter surgeon Simpson stage left * On quite the high from this sudden epiphany and my newfound status, I fished out a pair of old scissors and the sharpest knife from the cutlery drawer. I even gave them a bit of a rinse and a dip in my wine to 'sterilise' them. Oh yes, professional to the core.

I don't know if you have ever tried home surgery? I don't suppose you have. Well, I can tell you, it hurts. A lot. I'm not sure which hurt more the scissors or the knife. I decided I needed a stronger anaesthetic because the wine just wasn't cutting it. Excuse the pun. I shifted to gin. Straight. The gin helped enormously with the pain and my mood. I even found myself humming. Unfortunately, however, it didn't do my surgeon's eye much good. Things were getting kind of blurry and messy. After much hacking and snipping, there were blood and chunks everywhere. I was starting to feel a bit queasy. I reckoned I had rid myself of the offending 'body' though, so declared the operation a success. However, once I wiped the blood off, it became apparent that I hadn't really thought things through. I had expected just a gash in the skin, which would reseal itself through time, what I was confronted with was a different story altogether. I was peering into the vast depths of a mahooooosive gory crater! Unsure of how to proceed, I opted for the 'out of sight, out of mind' philosophy and stuck a whopping great plaster on it. There you go! It now looked clean, clinical and professional. Job well done. I toasted the successful operation with a large G and T and subsequently passed out. Only to wake again in the wee small hours, my wound burning and throbbing.. the bed sheets were soaked with sweat. Then came the terrible realisation of what I had done. I hardly dare look, but knew I had to. I peeled back the plaster hesitatingly. In the clear light of day, it looked like a battlefield. Flaming red, ragged and suppurating. Oh. My. Dog. It was obviously badly infected. Knowing my luck, I had probably contracted sepsis! Now I had no choice.

I was going to HAVE to go to the doctor. I managed to get an appointment almost straight away and in a panic tried to concoct a plausible story about how this had happened. I mean, I could hardly tell the truth! They would have me committed!

'So, erm, yes doctor, I was working in the forest, ahem, cutting down trees and *coughs*, I tripped over my axe and landed on a sharp branch (or the axe?) and there was blood everywhere. And, erm, then I called you, yes.' I could tell the doctor didn't believe me, but I was past caring. He prescribed me some antibiotics and referred me to the skin specialist. That's when it got VERY FRIGHTENING INDEED. The skin specialist took one look and told me he was going to have to operate straight away as 'it was too much of a risk to wait' I had waited for years before even doing anything!!!! I swear I nearly died on the spot. He did the surgery and sent a bit away for analysis. Can you imagine what the following week was like for me waiting for the results to come back? I couldn't believe my luck and still can't when the results came back clear... never, EVER, perform home surgery.

OH LORDY!

This photo is in lieu of Home Surgery photo...be thankful.

12

The Dutch Fetish

The Dutch Fetish

I seem to collect Dutch blokes. Not deliberately. Obviously. I am on my second and hope it ends there. Not that there's anything wrong with Dutch blokes. On the contrary....I just mean that I want to keep the one that I am on at the moment, coz I love him.

My first was considerably older than me. Maybe I also have a 'daddy thing'? Along with the apparent subconscious Dutch fetish. Who can say? Or maybe I again subconsciously veer towards the older man, as I somewhere deep down realise that I need adult supervision...Anyway, his name was Mr Clog. No, it REALLY was! Clog in Dutch (Klomp) We were together for sixteen years, the first five in France and after that in Holland. Sadly, he died. Oh no! It's not what you are thinking! It wasn't my fault! I didn't break him, I promise.

I didn't intend getting another Dutchman, or any man for that matter, it just happened. Along came Willem..... Also, older than me (the daddy thing again?????) He is lovely. He spoils me to bits (probably coz I am a princess ?) He does most of the housework, all the shopping AND all of the cooking. I am so lucky. He is a unique and inventive cook and is famous for, among other ingenious recipes, his brussel sprout pizza and the mahooooosive turkey the cooked in a wok when we were living on a boat. I bet all you ladies out there are seething with jealousy. Well, seethe away, coz he is mine and I ain't letting him go.

We met in Holland and lived on his sailboat for the first couple of years. He was to retire at fifty from the Dutch Navy and we decided that when he did, we would move to somewhere rural, in lovely nature. We both wrote down five countries where we would like to live and were pleasantly surprised that Norway was top of both our lists. Norway it was then. We didn't have much money, but didn't let that put us off. We scoured the internet looking for cheap properties below our meagre budget of fifty thousand pounds. Believe it or not, we managed to find ten, all in varying states of disrepair. We bought a raggedy old fold up caravan and chucked it behind our Defender and headed North.

Well......to cut a long story short, each property was worse than the one before and by the time we arrived at the last one we were getting desperate. We wanted to move NOW! The final house was very small but was the best of the bunch, so we just bought it and moved in just a few months later.

After living there for just over a year, we found that we loved Norway, but wanted more space, so it was back to scouring the Net.

Willem soon found us the house we now live in. A huge affair, with a good bit of land, on the island of Vesteralen. It was about six hundred miles North of where we were living and we couldn't afford to go and see it. Despite neither of us ever having been anywhere near that area in Norway, we just bought it online. What could possibly go wrong ???

Well....the day of the removal was here and the removal truck turned up. We had all the boxes ready and quickly helped load them into the lorry. Willem's shed, however, was the biggest job. He had all sorts of tools, generators, outboard motors, etc. etc. The removal guy asked him if he had emptied the petrol and diesel out of them.

Willem – 'No, they will be fine'

Removal man – 'I really would advise you to. If you don't, the insurance won't cover anything'

Willem –'Nah, it will be fine'

Removal man (muttering) – Your funeral....

So, we finished loading and the lorry set off on its long and treacherous trek, six hundred miles north, through snow and ice. We had a final clear up and packed just dog, cat and ourselves into the Defender and set out into the Blizzard to start our new lives 'Norway take 2'

The roads were slippery and the visibility poor, so we just took it nice and steady. The snow was flurrying down on the windscreen, but between the snowflakes, we could see what looked like an accident up ahead. There were flashing lights and lots of smoke.

'Oh no,' I said to Willem

'Some poor bugger has had an accident, in this awful weather'

As we got closer we could see that it was a lorry, from which the smoke was emanating. Closer still we could also see the flames! And........... writing .... on.....the.....side....of....the....lorry...

'VESTERALEN REMOVAL COMPANY'

OH

MY

DOG !!!!

It was OUR bleedin lorry !!!!

Willem pulled up alongside, where the removal man was

desperately shovelling snow onto the burning brakes of the truck. He offered to help, but the removal man said help was on its way. (He probably thought we had already jinxed him enough). He told us to drive on, which we did, taking one last look at the billowing smoke in the rearview mirror. Neither of us said anything, but we were both thinking the same thing,

'All our worldly goods are in that lorry!!! And they ain't fricking insured!!!!'

Well, worrying never solved anything, so we just continued on our way. We couldn't stay downhearted for long because Vesteralen was absolutely beautiful. We loved it from the word go. Lovely pointy mountains and glistening turquoise seas, it was paradise!

It's a good job we loved it because our problems had only just started. The estate agent didn't have keys to our new home, so we had to break a window and burgle our way inside. The house hadn't been lived in for years and was freezing cold and damp. The electrics didn't work and the pipes had frozen so we had no water. Not to worry!!! We had snow and plenty of it! The removal man phoned with both good and bad news. The good news was that they had managed to douse the fire before it spread and Willem's generator blew the frickin truck to smithereens. So our stuff was saved. Yayayyayayay !!! The bad news was that the truck was fecked and it was gonna take them ten days to get our stuff to us. Booooo !!!

So, we spent the next ten days in romantic candlelight, sleeping in our only set of clothes on the floor and drinking from water boiled from snow over a campfire! Willem sure knows how to show a girl a good time....

OH LORDY!

'Master Chef' Willem cooking on the sailboat

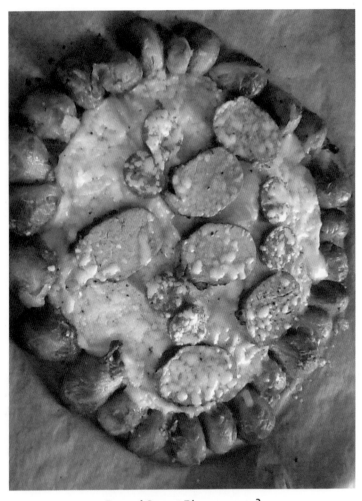

Brussel Sprout Pizza anyone?

13

Johnty Prayers

I want to share with you the popular Johnty prayers, the last of which I wrote, the others having been written by Torie. They are absolute classics. If you didn't know her, or you aren't a doggy person, feel free to skip over them.

JOHNTY PRAYER
My girlfriend, who art in Roffbury, Simonside be 'er name
The sun did come, weeze ad some fun
On da beach and in da sand dunes ;)
Give 'er dis day my gravy bones and forgive all my nortyness
Az ize forgive those who sniff round her botty
And lead her not into temptation
But deliver her from beagles
For mine is da blue girl, da cutest and da sweetest
Forever n Ever AMEN

JOHNTY PRAYER
My dad, who's out tonight, norty be thy name
My bed it come, my last chew nommed

In my tum and out my bum tomorrow
Give me tomorrow my grandma to play wiv
And let me not lead her into da temptation of custard creams
AMEN

JOHNTY PRAYER
My mammy, who's had a kebab, flabby be her bum
My dinner come and it was yum
From bowl to me tummy in seconds
Give all me pals a daily snuggle and forgive me for chewing
grandma's shoe
As I forgive 'er for calling ma an ickle bleeder
And lead me mate Benji border terrier away from norty eating
temptations
And deliver me friends away from achy pains
For ize be da cutest, most crinkle cut ears
Forever in dis home
AMEN

JOHNTY PRAYER
My mammy, who had a haircut, shorter be her mane
My day iz done, ize had some fun, in my field and in my garden
Give me tomorrow my daily gravy bone
And forgive me for trespassing in a cowpat
As I forgave mammy for trimming me winkle hair
Lead me not into sock chewing temptation
And deliver me from weasels
For mine is da settee, da bed 'n da pillows
For ever 'n ever
AMEN xxx

JOHNTY PRAYER

My great, great gran, who art in heaven, Ethel woz 'er name

She scrubbed her doorstep every day and liked to drink brown ale

Give all me pals their daily walk and forgive meeze for chasing the sparrows

As I forgive dem for poo splatting our windows

And lead me not into fox poo and deliver me from bath time

For mine iz me babble ball... not sharing me babble ball...

Forever MINE, always

AMEN xxx

JOHNTY PRAYER

My dad, who spilt red wine, ruined be his shirt

My mam did shout, got Vanish out...in a bowl den in da washer

Give rescue dogs a forever home and forgive me for jumping on Monty's head

As I forgive him for showing me his teggies...

And lead me not to the groomers and deliver me from fleabags..

For mine is da beef bone....not sharing me beef bone.. not ever...it's MINE

AMEN xxx

I hope Johnty doesn't mind, or that he doesn't sue me for plagiarism or copycat or anything, but I wrote my own Johnty prayer after his Mammy's passing. I hope you like it.

JOHNTY PRAYER (by me)
My mammy, who art in heaven, mammy Torie be her name
I still haff fun and my daily run
But wifout you it's just not the same
Give us this day, a way to cope
And forgive us our tears and crying
As we forgive them wot blub up against us
We know you iz wif Fred, snuggled on a cloud bed
And one day we will see each other again
Lead us not into tearfulness and deliver us from sadness
For ours is the memories, the love and the snoggin
Furever and ever
AMEN xxx

Ooh, maybe if I write a special prayer for Johnty, he will be less likely to take me to court? Let me think... yes, hopefully this should do the trick

JOHNTY PRAYER (by me)
Our pal, wot art in Long Clawson
Crinkle Ear be thy name
I nicked ya poems, had em published
On kindle and on paper
Give me this day, your understanding
Coz it's for the homeless doggies
Lead me not into destitution and deliver me from the bailiff
I'll give ya Ponky's tennis balls, all of her tennis balls
Forever and ever
AMEN

Beautiful Torie and Johnty

II

Part Two

14

Acknowledgements

I hope you enjoyed the book. At least it will have served the purpose of making you feel sane, if you doubt your sanity. If you did like it and want another, let me know....I have a FB page called OH LORDY.

I want to thank two people in particular, who made this possible. My editor, the lovely Geordie Macbagpipe, who tells me her real name is Anne Geall. We have been FB friends for nine years, but have yet to meet in person! I would love to go to Halifax, Nova Scotia and meet her. Maybe one day my impoverishment will come to an end and I will be able to visit.

Also my generous English friend Lynda Cottrell, who gave me a laptop to write the book on.*threatens* she too may be in for a visit...

Everydoggy needs an igloo and Border Bears!

Printed in Poland
by Amazon Fulfillment
Poland Sp. z o.o., Wrocław

60028014R00068